BAREFOOT IN MULLYNEENY

BAREFOOT IN MULLYNEENY

A Boy's Journey Towards Belonging

BRYAN GALLAGHER

HarperCollins*Publishers*

HarperCollins*Entertainment*
An imprint of HarperCollins*Publishers*
77–85 Fulham Palace Road,
Hammersmith, London W6 8JB

www.harpercollins.co.uk

Published by HarperCollins*Entertainment* 2005

2

A catalogue record for this book
is available from the British Library

ISBN 0 00 720405 1

Typeset in Sabon by Palimpsest Book Production Limited,
Polmont, Stirlingshire

Printed and bound in Great Britain by
Clays Limited, St Ives plc

As I write this, the memory of the tragic death of John Peel is still vivid in my mind. He changed the lives of many people with his encouragement, and he did that for me in his sincere appreciation of these stories. He broadcast some of them in his BBC programmes, and it was he who first broached the prospect of publication.

This book is respectfully dedicated to his memory.

Contents

INTRODUCTION

They say in this county where I was reared, that for six months of the year Lough Erne is in Fermanagh, and for six months, Fermanagh is in Lough Erne. The county is dominated by the vast stretches of the mighty lake. It is from its shores, and the surrounding countryside, that most of my stories come.

It is a beautiful county, with winding waters and rolling hills whose people have retained their own unique accent and the structure and tone of their speech. These people are the heroes of my stories. Their influences have shaped my awareness in so many ways: the gentle cadences of their way of speaking, and the lyricism of dialogue found nowhere else in the world; their courage in the face of adversity; their kindness and humanity, their wit and humour, the sturdiness with which they retain their folk culture; and of course their wonderful music. I spent my childhood among these people and I have never really left. It is my feeling that among the fields and the streets where you grew up, there your spirit will always live.

And there you will leave it when you die.

Bryan Gallagher, April 2005

BAREFOOT IN MULLYNEENY

The Map of Ireland

The sacrament of Confirmation is for ever associated in my mind with the town of Ballyhooley in County Cork. Not that I'm from Ballyhooley. I'm not from anywhere else on the south coast either. But I just cannot think, Bishop, Confirmation, without seeing the bottom half of that old school map – Carrantuohill and Dingle, Cahirciveen, the Blaskets and Courtmacsherry.

This has all to do with my primary school teacher many years ago. One of her methods of punishment was to put me standing out on the floor facing the wall where hung a map of Ireland. I often spent the best part of the day there. I can still remember the colours of the counties; Cork was pink, Tipperary was yellow, Queen's County was green and King's County was brown. I didn't know so much about the North, because you were supposed to look straight in front of you, and I was only a wee boy. But I occasionally stole a glimpse at my own beloved Lough Erne or Cushendall in the green glens of Antrim, far away, almost at the ceiling.

The year before my own confirmation, I was an altar boy at the ceremony. The bishop intoned the names of all the candidates.

'Con McManus.'

'Present.'

'John Maguire.'

'Present.'

And then on and on, until he came by mistake to my name. How my name came to be there I don't know, but it brought everything to a halt. There was a flurry of white clerical robes, great whisperings in the episcopal ear. And then canonical fingers pointing from all directions at *me*. I knelt in a state of trepidation akin to what the cat often felt on wet evenings before my mother gave it a boot out the door.

And then he called me over.

Over I went.

And he smiled. 'Ah,' he said, 'it is not the want of knowledge, it is the want of years.' He shook hands with me, and that was it.

Next day I breezed into school with the air of one

who has acquired some degree of greatness. But she was waiting for me.

'How many of you were at Confirmation yesterday?' she asked. All hands went up. 'Anybody notice anything wrong?' Nobody had. 'On the altar?' she prompted. Still nothing.

'What should you do,' she said slowly, 'when you shake hands with the bishop?'

'Kiss his ring,' we replied. And then a strange and awful feeling came on me.

'How many children saw a boy from this class shaking hands with the bishop yesterday?'

Everybody had.

'And did he kiss his lordship's ring?'

'No Miss.'

'No indeed,' she said venomously, 'no. Disgracing me opposite the whole parish.'

It was back to the corner. Face the wall. Ah well . . . Waterford is green . . . Ballyhooley is in Cork . . . Another long morning.

The Cobbler

I was six years old when I first met Jimmy the shoe-maker. We had just moved to the area and I was sent up to his workshop with a pair of shoes to be soled and heeled

'Come in,' he said as I hesitated at the door.

He worked in a small shed right alongside the road with a window of small dirty panes through which, as he told me himself, he could see out but nobody could see in. In any case, passers-by would have had to bend down to look inside, because the shop was on a lower level than the road. From inside you could see their feet and legs only, and Jimmy once told me he could identify most people by the sound of their footsteps.

'Your father has the best step of any man in this

country', he said to me. 'On a frosty night I could hear him coming half a mile away, quick and light in the hob-nailed boots'.

Huge shiny sides of leather were stacked along one wall, shoes in pairs, leather belts, harnesses hung on the other. A pot-bellied stove stood in the middle of the floor which he fed occasionally with off-cuts of leather or sods of turf from a pile at the back. The smoke had an exotic smell. A selection of knives sat on a shelf, blades curved or straight. I had never been in such an exciting place.

'What's your name?' he asked me on that first day.

'Bryan,' I replied.

'Bryan O'Linn had no britches to wear
He bought a sheepskin for to make him a pair
The hairy side out and the skinny side in
There's luck in odd numbers said Bryan o'Linn.'

He said.

And for all the years that I knew him, this was the name he called me.

I watched him at work, a shoe upside-down on the last before him, taking a handful of tacks from a box and putting them into his mouth, pushing them singly out through his lips ready to be taken in his left hand and hammered into the leather sole with his right. He worked with lightning speed.

Over the years I came to know him better. He had a

reputation for being irascible and acid-tongued, but for some reason he seemed to like me and we had a sort of mutual respect. Sometimes when I went in, he would greet me with a line of poetry that he remembered from his schooldays.

'*To be or not to be: that is the question,*' he would say, and then he would always add, 'But what the hell's the answer?'

Sometimes he would get things slightly wrong:
'*The curlew tolls the knell of parting day,*
The loving herd winds slowly o'er the lea . . .'
But I never told him that he wasn't quite accurate, because even though I was a schoolboy, I could see that he just loved language and the sound of words. If he liked you, he would stop work, take out his pipe, carve off a piece of plug tobacco with one of his razor-sharp knives, tease the tobacco in his hands, fill and light his pipe, spit in the fire, and talk.

'How is it,' he said one day, that there's no poets nowadays?' And then he recited for me 'The Burial of Sir John Moore':
'*Not a drum was heard, not a funeral note, as his corse to the rampart we hurried . . .*' He rolled the 'r's luxuriously over his tongue as he spoke, '*And he lay like a warrior taking his rest, with his martial cloak around him.*'

Word-perfect this time, right down to the last line:

'We carved not a line, and we raised not a stone, but we left him alone with his glory.'

He was also the local barber and on Saturday nights, in the dim light of an oil lamp, the shed would be full of men waiting to get their hair cut. His tongue was sometimes venomous about his customers.

'Phil McCaughey came in last night,' he said about one man who was slightly stooped and had a reputation for meanness, 'he came in with more humps on him than a bag of turf, that boy would skin a flea for sixpence.'

Of one man who had a long sharp nose, he said, 'He could split a hailstone with that nose of his.'

'So what are they teaching you in college,' he asked me one day.

I could not think of anything to say. Algebra, the Wars of the Roses, Boyle's Law, they all seemed so irrelevant in this man's company.

And then I thought of something I had read in an old school book of my father's, and I told him about Diogenes, and how he used to walk around Athens with a lantern in broad daylight, and when he was asked what he was doing, he said that he was looking for an honest man.

Jimmy said nothing and I wondered if he had understood.

A few days later he said to me, 'You can always tell the kind of a man by the footwear he leaves in,' and he started commenting on each pair of boots or shoes, refer-ring to them as people.

'That man is a dirty class of a person, look at the cowdung he didn't even bother to clean off the boots.'

'That man's lazy. He drags his feet. Look at the way the sole is worn.'

'That man is a show-off. He always gets the heaviest hobnails put in his boots to show how strong he is to be fit to carry them.'

'He is neat and tidy, clean shoes and good laces. And he's sensible,' said Jimmy.

He said to me one day, 'A man should always have a good pair of shoes and a good bed, because if he's not in one he's in the other.'

'And as for him!' He took a breath. 'Them's the best pair of shoes in the shop, and that's the third half-sole I put on for him, and he hasn't paid me one red cent yet. Your man Diogenes was right, and if he was round this country he'd need a searchlight not a lantern.'

His approach to religion was one of quiet scepticism. He always went to Sunday Mass where he knelt on one knee in the porch with his cap as a cushion for his knee. He was scathing about the quality of the preaching, but what he really appreciated was a good blood-and-thunder sermon, often delivered by a missioner.

He could repeat the content of the sermon almost

verbatim, and he would do so, frequently at night to his assembled court in the workshop.

'*Let me give you some idea of what eternity means,*' he would quote. '*Imagine a huge steel ball the size of this chapel. A little wren, a bird common in every Irish townland is flying through space. Once every hundred years, its wing brushes against the surface of the huge steel ball. That impact upon the steel ball would be light, you would say. Yet I tell you my dear brethren, that if this process went on and on through time until the steel ball was worn away by the touch of the wing, eternity would ONLY BE BEGINNING.*' He ended with a dramatic crescendo which always got a cheer from the audience. And then the questions would start:

'How could a wren live for a hundred years?'

'How could a wren breathe in space?'

I remember after a particularly dramatic sermon in which the priest promised damnation to all in the church who would not repent, there was a discussion about the nature of heaven.

One man who was a great footballer thought that it was a place where there would be matches every day.

Another man, a well-known fiddler, thought it would be a place where you could play music and swap tunes all day long.

Yet another, keen on dancing, said that there would be dances of all descriptions without ceasing.

Jimmy spat in the fire, looked at the last speaker, and said, 'Aye, you might be right, but from what we heard down there in the chapel, there mightn't be enough up there from this parish to make up a six hand reel!'

One night his stove chimney caught fire and the roof was burned down before the flames could be extinguished. Some people said that it was a judgement because of the blasphemous nature of the conversation. The missioner and the parish priest came to sympathise with Jimmy.

'Have you been attending the mission?' said one of them.

'Yes, I have.'

'Ah well, at least you have the grace of God about you,' said the priest.

'Not much good on a wet Saturday night, Father,' said the redoubtable Jimmy.

Many a morning at half past six, Jimmy would go off on his bicycle, a wooden mallet tied to the bar, and butcher knives in his pocket to do his other job, killing pigs for the local farmers. It was rumoured that he always carried a knife with him, even to Mass on Sunday. He was much in demand because he was fast, efficient and by the standards of the time, humane. He knew exactly where to hit the pig on the head with the mallet, so that it was immediately stunned and in seconds he had stabbed it in the heart so that as one man said to me, it was hanging up by the hind leg on a hook before it knew it was dead.

If a pig was restless and moving about, he would take off his cap and throw it on the ground. The pig would immediately go over to snuffle at it and bang went the mallet and it was business as usual. The pig was then butchered and stored in a tea chest packed with salt. After three weeks, Jimmy would go back to make sure that every part of the pig was getting properly salted, and to turn it if necessary.

He told me of two brothers who were noted for their prodigious appetites. He killed a pig for them and after three weeks, went back.

'What do you want?' said the brothers.

'I've come to turn the pig,' he said.

'Well you needn't have bothered your head,' they said, 'for we turned the last of it on the pan this morning.'

In addition to barbering and butchering, Jimmy had another little earner. He was small but also immensely strong. He would go down to the local shop and if there was a stranger there he would bet him ten shillings that he could 'Lift two six-and-fifties over his head'.

A six-and-fifty was an iron weight used for measuring out bags of meal or flour. It was, as the name suggests, fifty-six pounds, or four stone, or twenty-five kilos in weight, difficult to lift even one of them above your head. The stranger would invariably accept the bet, deceived by Jimmy's small stature. Jimmy would hoist the weights easily, clink them together above his head and leave with the money. He had no sympathy for the duped victim, merely saying, 'A fool and his money are easily parted.'

I remember being taken to a football match which has since gone down in legend in local folklore. Our local team was up against a team from the neighbouring parish. As in all local derbies there was fierce rivalry and in the preceding week the big lads at school spoke of little else. Jimmy and his brother were players on the local team.

The received wisdom was that Jimmy was 'a handy footballer but as wicked as a wasp' and that his brother, the goalkeeper, was 'quiet but dangerous when riz'.

A huge crowd from both factions was in attendance. They welcomed their heroes on to the field with wild and raucous tribal yells. Sure enough, after several minor scuffles, a full scale melee developed, the chief protagonists being the goalkeeper and a fearsome character from the opposing team who rejoiced in the nickname 'Stand Up' because this was his usual exhortation to his opponents when he knocked them down. I was too small to see exactly what happened but to my horror I saw Jimmy, my hero, running away. It was many years later that he told me the true story. Here are his words:

'Often times in a fight, men would come in from behind and it wasn't a fair contest. I could see this was going to happen here. I ran across to where I had left my clothes behind the whins when I was togging out, and got the butcher's knife. I tore back and straight into the middle of the pushing and shoving and I said, 'Take a look at that,' and showed them the knifeblade close under their noses. 'Stand in a ring,' I said, and I walked round it with the knife in my hand. 'The first man that interferes I'll gut him like a stuck pig, I said.

'The fight started. I knew our lad had a great left, and he hit him in what they call the solar plexus. Stand Up gasped and bent over and the red fellow (his brother) clinked him on the jaw and he went down. And that was that.'

'Would you have used the knife?' I asked.

'I would,' he said. 'Every man deserves fair play.'

I thought of the poet who said, 'Homer wrote *The Odyssey* about such a local row.'

The years went by and I noticed him getting slower, but his speech became even more picturesque. He would respond in a different way each time to the question, 'How are you?'

'So how are you, Jimmy?'

'Keepin' the best side out like the broken bowl on the dresser.'

'If I felt any better I'd have to see a doctor.'

'Still on the green side of the sod.'

'I'll shortly be making a load for four.'

14

'Movin' up in the queue.'

'Between the two big ones.'

'What two big ones?'

'Birth and death.'

And there I thought I had the key. These half-jocular poetic answers were his attempts to soften the terror of approaching death, a way of coping with a sense of a world beyond the grave.

I moved away to live in the town and it was some years before I saw him again. I had heard that he was going blind. He was sitting in the dim workshop, smoking his pipe. No leather, no shoes, no fire, alone.

'Hello, Jimmy,' I said. 'Do you know me?'

'I do,' he said, 'You have your father's voice.'

When I visited him in hospital, I walked past his bed at first. The nurses had cleaned up his smoke-blackened face, and I did not recognise this small pale frail little man, so vulnerable lying there. Was this the man who had hoisted a hundredweight so joyously over his head all those years ago? He opened his eyes and I could see that he knew me.

'Bryan O'Linn,' he said, and made an attempt to smile, 'How's Diogenes?'

'How are you, Jimmy?' I asked.

'It's a diggin' job,' he said.

The priest was generous at the funeral. 'He was a philosopher,' he said, 'an observer,' he said, 'he had a

great love of language and he had the ability to use it –
a fact which some people found out to their cost. His
workshop was a vernacular university of life, here was
a man who in another time could have been a great
professor.' And he finished with lines that I had often
heard Jimmy declaim from his roadside lectern:

> *Here he lies where he longed to be*
> *Home is the sailor, home from the sea*
> *And the hunter home from the hill*

And I thought, Jimmy, you know now what the hell's
the answer.

Jolly Nice

My uncle married a rich English widow who became my godmother. She was a lovely woman and regularly sent me books which I read voraciously. They had titles like *The Fifth Form at St Dominic's*, *Maitland Major and Minor* and *Tom Brown's Schooldays*. I became immersed in a world where boys talked about 'rugger' and 'the first eleven', and where if you were a 'cad' or a 'bounder' you were liable to get a sound thrashing in the boxing ring of the gym, where all fights were conducted with scrupulous fair play, with each boy having a second in his corner.

This ill-prepared me for life in a small village school in the Forties, and when I once had the misfortune to say that something was 'jolly nice', I was tormented unmercifully. There was one boy called Farrell about my own age who was noted as a great fighter. He was wiry, bony, and had fists as hard as stones. He was champion at Hardy Knuckles, and every time he fought, his opponent would be left cut and bleeding from fists that moved like lightning.

'Out of my way,' he would say when he came into school, and I would meekly obey, moving across the long desk to make room for him. I lived in mortal fear of him.

And then the bigger lads decided that it was my turn to fight him. I knew I was doomed when the first message arrived.

'Farrell says you're afraid,' they said.

'Tell him I'm not,' I said, lying.

'He says he can beat you with one hand behind his back.'

'Tell him he can try,' I said.

The fight was arranged for after school at the priest's gate, the one place where we would not be seen. I spent the night before in fear and dread, knowing I was in for a hammering. In vain I tried to cheer myself up by thinking what Maitland Major of the Lower Sixth would have done with his straight left.

Now I knew that various rituals were observed before a fight. A big fellow always held his arm out horizontally between the adversaries, saying, 'Best man spit over that arm,' then lowered it and the contest began. I decided that my only chance lay in surprise. No sooner was the arm lowered than, hysterical with fear, I hit him a ferocious haymaker on the right cheekbone.

'*A splendid left hook, delivered correctly with the knuckle part of the glove,' said Ponsonby of the Upper Third.'*

'A fierce box on the jaw,' said my schoolmates.

And that was it. It was all over. He ducked his head and grabbed me round the waist and I realized with a fierce joy that he was afraid. I thumped him on the back, and he refused to lift his head. We were pulled apart and I was declared the winner and while I was accepting the plaudits, Farrell hit me on the nose and the blood spurted out. But this was declared a 'false box' and he was chased away in ignominy. I went home covered in blood and glory.

Next day I said, 'Out of my way, Farrell,' and he moved. It was a six over the grandstand, it was the winning try at Twickers. And the feeling was indeed 'Jolly nice'.

I Dreamt I Dwelt in Marble Halls

It was always an adventure going to fetch the weekly can of buttermilk, taking the shortcut by the fields, crossing the footstick over the river, avoiding the neighbour's bull and eventually reaching the house. In truth it was little more than a hovel. The roof had fallen in at one end. Hens walked freely to and fro on the concrete floor. A calf nudged me gently in the back as I walked in the half-door.

The woman of the house always wore a man's hat from which protruded wisps of dirty grey hair. Her face had that grimy coal-miner's look from living in a smoke-filled atmosphere, but her churn was always spotlessly clean and when she gave me the buttermilk, she did it with an air of refinement and accepted the fourpence graciously. I gradually picked up snippets of information about her. She had been reared with nothing but the best, a piano in the house, carpets on the floor, music and elocution lessons and she had been the belle of the countryside, quite beautiful, dressed always in the latest fashion. On Sunday people would stop to look at her going to Mass in her pony and trap. Then her parents died and her brother started drinking himself to death and the farm to bankruptcy. There were rumours of a broken love affair, and gradually things had deteriorated into their present state.

One St Stephen's Day as I approached the house for the can of buttermilk I heard her singing. I stood near the dung-hill and listened. In a sweet quavering voice she was singing, 'I Dreamt I Dwelt in Marble Halls'. It was as startling as a cough in a graveyard.

I went up to the half-door and looked in. In her hessian bag apron she was standing with her back to me in the middle of the floor and she was singing to the empty hearth. She had her arms stretched out in front of her as if she were singing to her lover on the stage. I moved back a few steps and coughed to let her know I was there. The singing stopped and I went up to the door and knocked. She took the can from me without a word. The black of her face was wet and smudged where she had wiped it with her bag apron. I never told anyone about it and she never mentioned it to me.

The years went by. The buttermilk was fetched by younger brothers and sisters and I went away to college, but I was told she always asked about me. I intended visiting her, but with the carelessness of youth, I never did, and the next time I saw her was when I attended her wake. She had died in her sleep. Someone had whitewashed the bare walls of the room where she was laid out. It smelt of damp and lack of use. An old harmonium stood in the corner. The sun shone through the overgrown whitethorn hedge outside the small window and a tracery of shadows moved caressingly to and fro over the ruined face that had once turned all heads on a Sunday morning.

Her funeral was a wretched affair. Nobody stood to watch her make her last journey to the chapel. A neighbour and myself helped to carry the coffin. He had also dug the grave. The service in the graveyard was hurried and everyone left quickly but I stayed to help him fill in the sticky clay. I felt it was the least I could do.

When we had finished, we arranged the sods in a neat rectangular border around the heaped earth and he took off his cap and crossed himself, and wiped the sweat from his brow.

'Hard to imagine,' he said, after a pause, 'that there was one time when she could have had her pick of any man in the country.'

'So why did she never get married?' I asked.

And he told me about her one big love affair with a tall handsome policeman in the local barracks. He had been promoted to sergeant and transferred to another part of the country. He had written to her, asking her to marry him and she had replied, saying she would. She had given the letter to her brother to post, but he had torn it up and thrown it over the bridge into the river. Her words of love had floated away in a hundred pieces on the brown water and disappeared for ever into the dark depths of Lough Erne. And as I stood there, I could hear inside my head her sweet quavering voice and I knew now that it was the handsome face of a young policeman that she had seen in the dead ashes of the hearth when I had heard her singing all those years ago.

I had riches too great to count,
Could boast of a high ancestral name:
But I also dreamt which pleased me most,
That you loved me still the same,
That you loved me, you loved me still the same.

Clerical Error

When our new parish priest went to see his first local football match he let it be known to anyone who would listen that he was disgusted at the low standard of play. This was bad enough, but then he made a terrible mistake. He announced at Sunday Mass that he was going to bring a team of college boys and ex-college boys to play a special challenge match against the local Harps team.

'They will demonstrate the finer skills of Gaelic football,' he said.

The following Sunday the college boys arrived by bus, a thing unheard of in the Forties. They were immaculately togged out in proper football kit. Tall and lithe, they ran down the stony lane to the field fisting the ball to each other, taking great athletic leaps in the air and solo running with insolent ease.

Awaiting them were the men of the Harps. They had arrived on bicycles, still dressed in their Sunday suits. Many wore caps, and they were now togging out behind the whins that grew on the bank of the small river that flowed round the foot of the field. Off came the caps, then the upper-body clothing, coat, waistcoat, tie, detachable collar, shirt, vest. Some of them looked curiously like pandas, with sunburnt arms and necks contrasting with their fish-white bodies. Then it was on with the jersey, and immediately back on with the cap as if it were a protective talisman.

Legs that had not seen daylight since the previous match were revealed as the long johns came off, and behind the knees there was frequently a rich delta of alluvial dirt. Many wore their everyday socks supported below the knee by suspenders. These were men slowed by years of hard physical work but underneath the white skin, corded muscles rippled and they exuded an air of silent menace.

They didn't run on to the field. They walked, with the air of men who have an important parochial duty to perform, like taking up the Sunday collection. The crowd was the biggest ever seen at a local football match. They welcomed their heroes with wild yells. The excitement was tremendous. It was clear to all except the priest what was going to happen.

At the throw-in one of the college boys leaped like a salmon to catch the ball and was immediately pole-axed by a tremendous punch to the jaw. The team-mate who went to his assistance was kneed in the back. The referee, a local man, saw nothing wrong, and that in brief, was the story of the match. Flying solo runners would be tripped, they were hacked, kicked, bruised, battered.

Eventually the college boys could take it no longer. Many were country boys themselves and they retaliated. Fights broke out all over the field. Men turned their caps back to front and rushed to battle uttering heroic war-cries.

'Don't bother takin' off that jersey. I'll bate it off you!'

'I'll toss you where you stand!'

'I've knocked better men than you out of me way to get at a good man!'

The match was abandoned. The parish priest was given to dramatics. He rushed on to the soggy pitch, his galoshes splashing the pools of water. Standing amidst the carnage he raised his arms to heaven: 'My God! My God!' he said. 'Jesus, Mary and Joseph, what am I to say to the fathers and to the mothers of these young men I have brought here today?'

But one of the Harps, standing nearby, would have none of it. 'Ah for J-----s' sake what are you talkin' about, Father?' he said. 'Isn't there two of our men lyin' dead in the river!'

27

Last of the Islandmen

I have a boat, fibreglass with a big engine at the back, and I often sail up Lough Erne past the island of Inishlught, which means 'the island of the people'. I was taken there once, many years ago when I was six and a half years of age. The woman who lived there with her brother collected me from school by arrangement with my parents. She came on her old-fashioned bicycle with two bags of shopping on the handlebars and she seated me on the carrier behind the saddle, short legs dangling from either side.

'Mind the spokes,' she said as we wobbled off.

The road was rutted and made of gravel and when we came to steep hills, she walked, wheeling the bike, and keeping up a constant flow of conversation. To this day

I can never travel that road without hearing her voice as she looked over the rushy fields and named the townlands we passed through: Kilnakelly, Coragh, Tirraroe, Coratistune, Dragh and Cornanoe. They were like poetry in my mind. The road became narrower with a mane of green grass up the centre and finally round a bend it ran straight down into the lake and I could see it sloping away underneath the water.

'I'll just give Tommy a shout,' she said. 'Tommeee,' she yelled. Sound travels well on water, she explained. Out of nowhere, it seemed, a boat came. The oarsman shipped his oars and got out. Nobody spoke. He lifted the two bags of shopping into the boat and looked down at me. He was huge.

'Were you ever in a boat before?' he asked.

'No,' I said.

'Are you afraid?'

'No.'

'Good lad,' he said, and he picked me up under one arm, and stepped into the boat. 'Sit at the end,' he said.

His sister pushed us off, stepping easily aboard as the boat floated. Maybe it was the contrast with the bumpy bike ride but I had never experienced such a sensation, smooth, velvety, silken, gentle. And then he started to row. With every one of his mighty strokes I could feel the boat surge forward. It was years later when I next felt the same sensation in a boat only this time there were eight of us rowing in a sleek university racing craft, not the heavy wooden boat with a lone oarsman taking us to his home in Inishlught, the island of the people.

We walked up a cobbled green lane and in through the half-door into the kitchen. There was no ceiling and I looked up at the smoke-blackened rafters supporting the scraws of turf which carried the thatch, with the pointed ends of the hazel scollops sticking through them, holding the thatch as a hairpin holds a woman's hair.

I sat at the oilcloth-covered table. She busied herself unpacking the shopping while he took a round black pot and carved off, yes, carved off a chunk of solid porridge, put it in a bowl with some milk and ate it. He saw me looking at him.

'Do you want some?' he asked. I hated porridge and never ate it at home.

'Yes,' I said.

He handed me another bowl and spoon. I ate every bit and scraped the bowl with the spoon as I had seen him do.

'Would you like to go outside and look around?' they said.

I knew they wanted to talk privately and I obeyed. The hens came around me expecting to be fed, and one of them stood between my feet, and a calf nudged me gently in the back. A black and white collie sat on the ground at my knee. In the distance, there were two islands, close together with a passage in between them. In that light they seemed to float above the horizon and I knew that the passage led to Tir-na-nOg.

There is a line in Tennyson's 'Ulysses' which says:

> . . . All experience is an arch wherethro'
> Gleams that untravelled world whose margin fades
> For ever and for ever when I move . . .

When I read that for the first time I thought of the passage between those two islands with a glimpse of the lake beyond, seeming to go on and on for ever. It was so quiet that when a fish jumped in the water, I jumped too. I wanted the day never to end.

When we got back to the mainland, he lifted me out.

'You're a toppin' wee lad,' he said. 'We'll make a lough man of you yet.'

That night in bed my mind was full of images of what I had seen, and I fell asleep dreaming of water lapping at the bow of the boat, and water hens with their quick jerky movements among reeds bending in the breeze, and tall herons standing so still you could hardly see them, and supercilious swans gliding disdainfully out of the way of the boat, and the road disappearing under the green water leading to some mysterious underwater kingdom, and the passage between the islands that led to fairyland.

Nobody lives now on the island of the people. Just one sad ivy-covered gable remains of the house where myself and the big man ate the porridge. Tommy the boatman lies under six feet of clay in Knockninny graveyard and I regret that I never told him – I never once told him of the wondrous, magical day that he gave a young boy half a long century ago.

Yes, I have a boat of my own now, fibreglass, with a big engine on the back, but I have never been able to bring myself to visit that island ever again.

Goodbye Dolly Gray

All our class successfully negotiated our way through our first confession and communion, and next day, in the odour of sanctity, we were allowed to have a school concert. There was a prize of sixpence for the best singer. One girl sang 'The Old Bog Road', a sad song about an emigrant thinking of his homeland. Another sang 'Teddy O'Neill', about a girl lamenting the departure of her boyfriend. I thought, in view of the day that was in it, I would sing something lively, so I launched into 'Goodbye Dolly Gray'.

Goodbye Dolly I must leave you, though it breaks
my heart to go.
Something tells me I am needed, at the front to fight
the foe.

See the soldier boys are marching, and I can no longer stay,
Hark, I hear the bugle calling, Goodbye Dolly Gray.

I had heard my mother singing it to herself and I had no trouble picking it up. I gave a spirited rendition, and when I saw the other children tapping their feet in time to the music, I figured that the sixpence was as good as mine. I finished, and flushed with success, I sat down in triumph. Alas, pride goes before a fall. The teacher looked at me witheringly.

'A most unsuitable song,' she said. 'That is a British army marching song, next child to sing please,' and added in an undertone to the big girls, 'what else would you expect from a policeman's son?'

When I told my mother, she laughed and said, 'She's right. It is a British army marching song. Next time you better sing "Wrap the Green Flag Round Me Boys".'

And the remarkable thing is that I could have done so easily, because in our house, when I was growing up, we were 'exposed to a wide range of musical experience', as the teaching manuals have it. My mother had what seemed a limitless repertoire, ranging from Irish traditional music to Victorian music hall and Moore's Melodies, and from hit tunes of the Forties to light opera, and the singing of Tauber, Gigli and above all, John McCormack, who was revered by my parents as a musical deity.

Music was almost a way of life. One of my earliest memories is of my mother, playing the piano and singing in her fine round voice, 'I Dreamt that I Dwelt in Marble Halls'.

Once a week, a lady used to arrive at our house on a bicycle to teach us the piano. The sole purpose of this seemed to be to pass music exams, and enjoyment did not enter into it. Studies, scales major and minor, in similar or contrary motion, sight-reading and ear tests were the order of the day. I cordially hated these lessons, and instead of practising, spent my time picking out tunes by ear, much to the teacher's displeasure. One day, as I came into the room for my lesson, she said, 'Don't look over. What chord is this?'

She played a chord on the piano. 'A flat,' I replied

'What note is this?' she asked, and played a note near the top of the piano.

'F sharp,' I replied without hesitation.

'You have perfect pitch,' she said. 'You should be doing far better.'

Full of pride, I told the boys in school, but I would have been better not to, because one of them told the teacher that I had used bad language and said she was a 'perfect bitch', and I was put standing out on the floor for the rest of the day.

However, my musical interest increased, and I dug out every songbook in the house and learned the words as well as the notes. One that sticks in my mind was 'The Bridle Hanging on the Wall', about a man whose favourite horse had died.

> *There's a bridle hanging on the wall*
> *There's a saddle in the empty stall*
> *No more he'll answer to my call*
> *There's a bridle hanging on the wall.*

I must have been a soppy kind of child, because I used to have tears in my eyes when I sang this and just wallowed in the sentimentality. Looking back, the only excuse I can have for this mawkish behaviour is that I myself had known and ridden a neighbour's beautiful white horse which had died under tragic circumstances.

I remember about this time making my stage debut, singing at a parochial concert. During the holy season of Lent, no dancing was permitted by the Church, and the principal entertainments were the parish concerts. The parish priest had a simple plan of action for these affairs. He would come out on to the stage, look down at the audience, and call somebody up to perform. Refusing was not an option. 'Paddy Gunn, come up and play the accordion,' he would say. 'John McManus, come up and play the fiddle.'

One night he called out, 'Janey Maguire for a song.' And Janey, from a well-known musical family, came up and sang 'By Killarney's Lakes and Fells', and received warm applause. After a few more items, the priest called out, 'Ownie Maguire for a song.' Ownie was Janey's brother, and he sang 'By Killarney's Lakes and Fells', and received slightly more tepid applause.

Later on, Alsie Maguire from the same family was called upon and when she sang the same song, the audience were getting restive and there were a few shouts. There were six Maguires and they all sang 'By Killarney's Lakes and Fells'. As soon as the last one started the first line, the audience, who were by now expecting it, yelled, shouted and cheered wildly. The parish priest, who was both tone-deaf and naïve, was highly gratified by the reception.

Sometimes members of the local dance band would perform as guest artistes and I used to look in awe at these celebrities, with drum kit, double bass, saxophones and with microphones powered by a car battery. There was much arranging of wires and stands and loudspeakers on the stage, all watched with the greatest of interest by us, the audience. Then we heard a crackling sound through the speakers, and a band member came out on the stage, tapped the microphone, and said into it, 'Hello, hello.'

We responded, 'Hello, hello,' as good manners dictated, so that there was instant dialogue across the footlights.

Man:	Hello!
Audience:	*Hello!*
Man:	Testing! Testing!
Audience:	*Testing, testing!*
Man:	Testing, one, two, three.
Audience:	*Testing, four, five, six.*

I thought that this band was the pinnacle of sophistication, and when they started their programme, with the leader saying in a slightly American accent, 'Ladies and gentlemen, welcome to the music of the Starlight dance band,' and when they described the songs as 'numbers', and used the word 'entitled', I thought, 'This is really showbusiness.'

'We'd like to play a number entitled "South of the Border down Mexico Way",' they would say. And the singer wasn't a singer, but a 'crooner'. They sat down behind music stands with sheet music on them, and SL painted on the front. 'And here is our crooner John to sing for you our next number, "Cruising Down the River".' The drummer counted aloud in waltz time, 'With a one two three, two two three,' and they started.

I was in heaven.

Mrs Malaprop and Daughter

It all started when the woman was getting married. She lived on a poor hungry farm on the side of the mountain in the Thirties. Money was scarce in the household and everybody in the family was trying, as they say, to pull the divil by the tail. But, poor as they were, for them the most important thing in life was to keep up appearances opposite the neighbours. Now in those days, very few people in the country would have had cars, just the doctor, the parish priest and the local big shop-keeper. If you had a car at a wedding, it was indeed a grand affair, but if you had two cars, then it was the talk of the countryside.

On the morning of her wedding, there was a light fall of snow on the ground. She got out the wheelbarrow and pushed it backwards and forwards over the snow to leave wheel tracks, so that the neighbours would think that she had cars at the wedding. Ever after that, instead of Margaret, her real name, she was known in the countryside as Maggie the Barrow.

The offspring of the union was first a boy and then a girl, who arrived many years afterwards. 'The shakin's of the bag,' as the local miller described it. The poor husband, a decent hardworking man, died shortly afterwards, from shock, some said. Others said that it was from constant harassment about his accent, his appearance and his language.

When a like-minded woman friend had said to her one day, 'I heard your husband in the shop the other day saying that he was going for a cartload of "dung". I am surprised that you allow him to use such coarse language,' she had replied, 'If you only knew the trouble I had getting him to call it that!'

Sadly for her, the boy turned out to be a wastrel, a lazy, slothful drunkard. She had a dreadful job covering up his misdeeds, and she was delighted when he announced that he was going to America. It was a time of emigration, and Enniskillen railway station was often the scene of harrowing farewells. When she saw how lonely all the other women were, parting with their children, she thought that she had better put on some sort of show, so she started lamenting.

'Oh now, amn't I the sad and broken woman today with my fine son going from me across the ocean to Amerikay . . .' But like all of us when we don't mean something, she was inclined to overdo it. '. . . and who will cut the turf for me, and win the hay for me and plant the crop for me, now that my pride and joy is leaving!'

And when she went on just a bit too long, the son, sitting in the railway carriage listening, got up and walked back on to the platform and said, 'Ah sure, if you think that much of me, Mother, I won't go at all.'

And he went down the town and into the first public house and drank all the money that his mother had given him for his passage. Everyone's patience wears out, and shortly afterwards, a couple of his uncles, big mountainy men, had a quiet chat with him and he left rather hurriedly for England. His mother announced that he had gone across the ocean to the town of England to take up a very good job. Meanwhile, her daughter Biddy had arrived at our school, and it was clear from the outset that she was following in her mother's footsteps and that she too had pretensions to refinement.

The first we knew of it was when she informed everybody that her name was not Biddy but Brigid. The mistress was a spiteful kind of a woman and called her Biddy at every opportunity, but the master was a more understanding man and decreed that she should be called Brigid, so Brigid it was. But unofficially, and out of her hearing, all the boys called her 'Biddy the Barrow'. She had by now adopted a sort of falsetto voice and had done her best to iron out the local accent that we all possessed.

One day the master gave us a composition entitled 'A Day Out' and we had to read aloud our finished efforts. We stumbled through them as best we could. One boy's day out was when he took the cow to the bull; another boy took the horse to the forge to get shod; a girl went picking blackberries with her friends. Now someone had obviously told Brigid that you didn't say runnin' and jumpin' and walkin'. You pronounced your -ings. You said walk*ing*, and runn*ing* and jump*ing*.

When it came to her turn, she stood up and in her ghastly falsetto voice she read, 'We went for the day to *Bundoring*. We passed through *Enniskilling* and we had *mutting* for tea.'

Strangely enough nobody laughed although one boy muttered rather unkindly that the only time she saw Bundoran (a seaside resort frequented by well-off people) was on a map and that it was far from mutton that she was reared, and another wondered where did she park the barrow when she was having the tea.

But it was after she left school that her sayings became legendary. She went into the shop and asked for, 'Ay pound of morgarine and a half a pound of biscakes please.' When a local man moved away from the area to live in the town, she said that he was 'presiding on the outerskirts of Enniskilling'.

She announced grandly in the shop, when her uncle bought a new car, that he had purchased a Ford *Concertina*. (Somebody added that she had also declared that it had reversing lights front and back, but this last part was apocryphal.) However she did talk about looking out at the scenery through the *windowscreen*.

When the grants became available for farmers to replace their wooden gates with metal ones, she sailed into the same shop and asked if they had any *tubercular steel gates*. And when that shop was converted into a supermarket she declared, 'There's no money in the country since they opened the *Common Market*.'

But her finest hour came during the height of the troubles. There was always army activity in our area, particularly on the mountain where she lived because it actually straddled the border. One morning she came down to the shop and announced, 'The security forces were busy last night. They threw an *accordion* round the entire mountain.'

Altar Altercation

I always thought that the Latin Mass was much more exciting for altar boys than the modern equivalent. The priest had his back to you and couldn't really see what went on behind him. There was always competition among the altar boys to see who would kneel on the right-hand side of the altar because that was where the action was. The boy serving right, as it was called, would be the first to walk out on to the altar, he would go up and change the missal from one side of the altar to the other before the gospel, he would ring the bell at the more solemn parts of the Mass, and at the offertory he served the wine and water to the priest.

The boy serving left had nothing to do except at communion time when he would hold the paten under the chins of the communicants as the priest put the sacred host on their tongues. In the sacristy before Mass there would be arguments and frequently fisticuffs to decide who was serving right. It reached such a pitch that the priest made a rule that whoever was in first would serve right. But then boys started coming earlier and earlier until once a boy arrived to serve eleven o'clock Mass as the people were coming out of the half-past-eight Mass. So the law was amended; no boy should arrive earlier than half an hour before Mass began.

One Sunday I set off to serve Mass. My partner that day was Gerry. He was a wiry little fellow whose father was a veteran of the First World War and had a wooden leg. He was a noted fighting man and all the neighbours were afraid of him.

As I was coming up the road to the chapel I saw Gerry coming down. He saw me and we both started to run. Neck and neck we ran over the chapel lane and in the gate. We couldn't run inside the chapel because there were early worshippers there but we walked briskly side by side up the aisle, genuflected together at the altar rails and jammed in the vestry door, neither of us giving an inch. We each claimed to have been in first. While the priest was vesting, we wrestled behind his back and eventually I got myself in pole position.

The routine was that the boy serving right would walk out first and stop when he came to his position. The other boy would walk past him over to the left. This time when I stopped, Gerry planted his two hands in my back and gave me a violent push so that I staggered over to the left side of the altar leaving him in sole possession of the field. When he went up to change the missal I moved over to the right. When he came back he knelt beside me so that the two of us were on the same side. I grabbed the beater for the bell and went over to the left.

'I have the beater,' I said across to him. 'You can't ring the bell.'

'I have the bell,' he said, 'and if you don't give me that bloody beater, I'll ring it with my knuckles.'

I never thought he would, but he did. Mind you, instead of a sonorous dong, dong, dong, it sounded a reedy ding, ding, ding, and the priest glanced round. When we went up to hold up the priest's chasuble at the consecration, we elbowed each other viciously in the ribs. Gerry's father had special permission to receive communion standing up because of his wooden leg. When I held the paten under his chin, he glared balefully at me down his nose as he opened his mouth to receive and he shook his fist at me as the priest and I moved to the next communicant.

During the reading of the public notices, the altar boys turned round to face the congregation, reclining gracefully with our elbows on the steps. I heard not one of the priest's words for there he was in the front seat, wooden leg stretched out in front of him, shaking his fist at me and drawing his finger meaningfully across his throat.

When Mass was over I went out the back door of the chapel and home across the fields to escape him. My shoes were covered in muck and I got hammered by my father for my carry-on on the altar and for ruining my good shoes. The only consolation I had was that when Gerry and I fought in school the next day all the big lads said that it was the best fight they had seen in years.

Sand Pit

If you travel around a certain area of the district where I was reared, you will see the landscape pockmarked with craters like the pictures of the surface of Mars. Here and there, crooked pillars of earth stand like the rock stacks of the Orkneys. Pools of stagnant water lie all around. You are looking at the remains of a time when the place was alive with lorries, tractors, horses and carts and men, all digging for sand. The impetus for this explosion of activity was the building of an aerodrome in the nearby town of Enniskillen during the Second World War. It required enormous quantities of sand and ours was the only convenient area where it could be obtained.

The method was simple. A lorry was backed up close to the face of the pit and men started shovelling the sand from the base into the lorry. The face of the pit was often as high as sixty feet and they cut into the base so that the face was undermined and new sand fell down from the top. This sand was loose and easier to fill into the lorries. It was backbreaking, monotonous work, shovelful after shovelful of heavy sand having to be pitched up in the air over the high sides of the lorry, hour after hour, day after day. One lorry filled, drove away, another reversed in. They laboured in heavy rain and in crucifying heat, but work was scarce and any job, even one that paid subsistence wages, was welcome.

I often did it myself. It was highly dangerous, because sometimes a slip of sand would come unexpectedly and you had to be quick to run out of the way. Once it happened to me and I ran with an avalanche of sand seeming to follow me. It was a minor slip and only reached my knees, but I remember the awful sensation of standing there trying to run but unable to move.

Then one day, a gang of men were working in one of the pits when a movement occurred in the face high above their heads. Forty feet up, the sand parted. A crack appeared, spreading jaggedly across from left to right, slowly widening like a terrible opening mouth. The men looked up, rooted with fear. But one man didn't. He stood with his back against the face, spread his arms out wide as if he could hold back the sand and shouted, 'Run, boys, run!'

And they did, fleeing for their lives. The top of the cliff of sand collapsed with a sighing sound. It was over in seconds. There was a dreadful silence. They rushed back and started shovelling frantically. There was no talk, no shouting, just a quiet desperation as they strove to save him. One man, his brother, was making thin mewling sounds as he worked.

'Careful boys,' said the foreman, 'watch for his head.'

Then there was a shout, 'There's his cap!'

They could just see his head underneath. But then another shout of, 'Run, run!' as yet another jagged crack appeared, and a second deadly shower of sand rained down on them as they fled.

They went back and shovelled doggedly until they uncovered the body, lifted his limp form out of the sand that had killed him, and laid him down gently. They put coats under his head for a pillow and crossed his arms over his chest. They stood around, took off their caps and blessed themselves as they looked down at his life-less body. Somebody went for the doctor and the priest.

He was brought in the back of the lorry to the barracks where my father was the sergeant. I remember watching from an upstairs window. Men were sitting around him on the sides of the lorry. His brother was one of them, clutching the dead man's cap in his hands; the corpse still wore his wellingtons. A small crowd had gathered and crossed themselves as the lorry drove past. Some time later, a woman went up to the barracks. She was crying, the dead man's wife. Then a hearse went up with a coffin in it. My father sat in grim silence at the lunch table that day and my mother said, 'We'll say a prayer for the man that is dead, and all belonging to him, God help them.'

I have often wondered what passed through the man's mind that day when he stood with his back to the deadly avalanche of sand, arms outstretched as in a crucifixion, making a last noble, defiant, but futile gesture to save his comrades before going to meet his Maker.

Nobody worked in the pits the next day, nor on the day of the funeral, but after that, it was work as usual. There was no time for sentiment. Contracts had to be fulfilled and families fed.

Requiem for a Huntsman

My first funeral as a seven-year-old altar server was memorable. I was standing by the graveside holding the holy water for the priest to sprinkle on the coffin, when a hare dashed through the mourners, leaped over the open grave and out through the chapel gate. Through the hedge at the foot of the graveyard, two hounds appeared, barking and giving tongue, and finally we could hear hallooing and cheering and a man burst through, following the hunt. When he came level with the funeral, he took off his cap, blessed himself, said 'Well, Father,' went out the gate and immediately started cheering and hallooing again.

Everybody smiled, even the priest and chief mourners, because P. was a legendary huntsman and everyone understood his passion for the sport. In a different capacity, he was also involved in another funeral at which I was again the altar server.

It was the custom of the time that the crowd remained by the graveside, reciting the rosary as the grave was filled in by the gravediggers. P., a noted worker, was chief filler-in. At first, the sticky clay fell heavily and hollowly on the coffin, then the sound gradually softened to dull wet squelches as the grave filled up. The work was brutally hard, but P. revelled in it. Off came his coat as he warmed to his work, then his waistcoat, then he opened his collar at the neck as with shovel and graip he moved the heap of clay, bit by bit into the grave.

All this while, the rosary was being recited by the mourners, the drone of the Hail Marys and Holy Marys the sound backdrop to P.'s grunting strength. 'Holy Mary, mother of God pray for us sinners now and at the hour of our death.'

'Amen,' said P. and then suddenly he beat frantically at his face. 'Isn't the graveyard wide enough for you, you bastard!' he roared. A wasp had stung him in the face.

The rosary continued haltingly, and P. finished the job, arranged all the sods in a neat rectangle around the grave, then stood and surveyed his work for a moment. Then he hit the top of the heaped clay with the flat back of the shovel and said, 'There ye boy ye, you'll not get out of that!'

*   *   *

Fifty years on and I was attending his funeral. The church was packed and I had to stand outside with the local huntsmen who were to form a guard of honour. The priest spoke warmly about him, his love of sport, how he was a fearless footballer with no regard for his own safety, nor, he added, for the safety of others. The old warriors around me looked at each other and smiled grimly.

'P. was baptized here in this church,' he said, 'confirmed here, married here and it is in these grounds he will be laid to rest beneath the earth over which he loved to hunt.'

His coffin was carried on the bony shoulders of his comrades, led by the priest and followed by two men with beagle hounds straining forward at the leash. One carried a hunting horn. They retreated up to the top of the hill behind the graveyard where they stood silent and still during the burial ceremonies, silhouetted against the skyline, the wind whipping the skirts of their coats, and just for an instant, I could imagine I was looking at Finn and Oisin, the heroes of Irish legend with their great wolfhounds Bran and Sgeolan.

When the prayers were finished one of them put the horn to his lips and blew a long, long blast that carried on the wind over the graveyard and across the fields below.

The hedges were now cut back neatly, the grass was

a lush green and there were no rushes or whins or briars to shelter a fox or hare, but I could still make out the spot where he had burst through the hedge more than half a century before and I could follow the track where my seven-year-old eyes had seen him walk out the gate with his long huntsman's stride.

And then as I looked, one of the two men on the hill raised the arm with the horn high over his head, a final salute to a dead comrade, and men and dogs disappeared over the skyline. There was a moment of silence in the graveyard and then, like a film that is re-run, once again everybody smiled, even the priest and the chief mourners smiled, and they chatted and laughed and talked about the mighty deeds of the man who was gone.

P. would have liked that.

Oremus

The first man I ever saw laughing till the tears ran down his cheeks was our parish priest when I was six and a half years old. He was a huge man and when he cycled down the road, straight-backed on his high bicycle, you could always see his white head above the tall hedges gliding along like a huge disembodied egg. He was a former county footballer and when he visited our school he would stand in front of the class and say, 'Can you say the Hail Holy Queen in one breath? I can.' And then he would proceed to do so.

'Sixty yards with either foot,' he would say. 'Sixty yards with either foot.' I had no idea what he was talking about, most of the time.

I was a precocious reader and even at that age I had

already devoured any books I could lay my hands on in the house, including old schoolbooks belonging to my parents. I read about Whang the Miller who was avaricious, and the Village Blacksmith, the muscles of whose brawny arms were strong as iron bands, and Roman legends about the twins Romulus and Remus who were suckled by a she-wolf and how Horatius kept the bridge in the brave days of old.

It was decided I should become an altar boy. My mother taught me all the Latin and I made my debut under the care of the established older boys. Their Latin was different from mine, they said it very fast and it seemed to bear no relationship to what was written in the prayer book. But I was in awe of these hardened warriors and did my best to imitate them, much to the displeasure of my mother who described it as incomprehensible gibberish. Then came the morning when I served Mass alone for the first time.

'Read the Latin properly,' the priest said, as we proceeded to the altar.

Now this priest loved Latin. He carved the words out of the air with great love, and I suppose incomprehensible gibberish would have offended him.

After the first response, he bent down and said again, 'Read the Latin properly,' and I did, or at least I tried.

'*Ad deum qui laetificat juventutem meam,*' I said, and '*Confiteor Deo omnipotenti* etc. etc.'

Now every few minutes, I noticed him saying, '*Oremus*,' which I now know means, 'Let us pray.' Then he would bow slightly towards the centre of the altar and pause. I thought I should be saying something in response and that this bow was a signal to me to do so.

The next time he said '*Oremus*,' I replied, '*O Romulus*.' And I repeated it every time. '*Oremus*,' said he, '*O Romulus*,' said I.

When I got home, the kitchen was darkened with the huge shape of the parish priest. The tears were streaming down his face, my father was doubled-up laughing, and my mother was smiling over the breakfast range. Nobody said a word to me as I passed through. My father told me later that '*Oremus*' did not require a response.

Rite of Passage

I'll never forget the first time I went out with the mummers back in the late Forties, because it was then I had one of those turning points that occur in everyone's life. I was much younger than the rest, still at primary school, but I was taken along because I could play the flute. We assembled for instruction in the house of an old man, himself a former mummer. He showed us how to make the conical straw hats and told us that on no account must we let our faces be seen. He seemed to think that this was most important for mummers. Then he taught us the rhymes. I longed to be the captain with his clarion call. *Room, room, gallant boys, give us room to rhyme And act out our activities for this is Christmas time.*

Or Beelzebub with his rhythmic verse. *Here comes I*

Beelzebub, And over me shoulder I carry me club, And in me hand a drippin' pan, Amn't I a jolly old man.

By the light of a hurricane lamp in the hayshed we sat round working at the straw while he told us stories of his own mumming exploits.

'There was one Christmas,' he said, 'when all the boys were laid up with the flu except me. And I decided to go out alone. I used to knock at the door, play a bit of music outside in the dark, say all the rhymes in different voices, and then at the end go up to the door and say we didn't want to disturb the house going in. This worked well until I came to the house of a grand woman who was also noted for her meanness. When I had finished, she put her head out the door and said in her grand voice, "Wonderful, wonderful, and now come forward and I will give a penny to each member of the troupe."'

Now I had a friend at school – at least, I thought he was a friend. In the strictest confidence, I told him that I was going out mumming that night and that we would be visiting his house. The kitchen was crowded when we went in. We launched straight into our performance. Everybody became involved, laughing and tapping their feet. And then, in the middle of the dance, my best friend stole round behind me and knocked my straw hat off.

That moment is still seared in my mind. Everything stopped, the music, the cups halfway to mouths, and all eyes turned to me. The mummers' straw hats turned to me and, like a spectator, I saw myself, a small bareheaded boy holding a flute, surrounded by huge figures whose straw hats reached to the ceiling.

There was total silence. And then a strange thing happened. Nobody laughed, and slowly everyone shifted their attention to the smirking face of my best friend. And as I too turned round, I saw the smile slowly fade as he realized he had made a dreadful mistake. I retrieved my hat and resumed the music.

As we were going out, his father slapped me hard on the back, put a shilling in my hand and said, 'You're a powerful gosson. You're a great mummer.'

And walking with the others into the darkness, I was dimly aware that I had become part of something that was very important.

The Huntsman

They say that dogs become like their owners, and the two beagle hounds that came lolloping down the lane had a tail-wagging greeting for me and walked tongue out by my side to the old huntsman's door.

'You've come for the spuds,' he said, and we headed over the fields to the potato pit. With a spade, he broke the frozen soil covering and removed the straw to reveal the heaped potatoes.

'Don't dirty your hands,' he said, 'just hold the bag.'

The dogs licked my hands as I crouched down. His own big hands moved with surprising delicacy and speed as he filled the potatoes. He tied the bag and hoisted it effortlessly on to his shoulder, stepping easily over a wide drain on his way back to the house.

I had heard about himself and his brother who lived here high up on the mountain. They were simple men, and for entertainment they would go to Mass in a different town each Sunday morning, leaving the house at five o'clock in the morning and crossing the mountain on foot, and they would spend the rest of the week talking about what they had seen. At Christmas time they walked fifteen miles to the monastery outside Enniskillen to go to confession.

When the first moving pictures came to the local hall the films were all Westerns. One night the two brothers went along. In the film there was a cattle stampede straight at the camera. One of the brothers ran outside for fear of being trampled. The other stayed, but at the end, he went up and looked behind the screen to see where the cattle were coming from.

One brother did the cooking and had papered the walls with pages from the *Beano*. The other did the outside work, but his consuming passion was hunting. I asked him where was the furthest he had gone to hunt. He told me he had once gone to the big St Stephen's Day hunt in Dundalk.

'Over them hills there,' he said, pointing to the east, 'and through the County Monaghan.' It was going to be his big adventure and there would be weeks talking in it. It took him three days walking and he slept in haysheds on the way, lying between his two dogs for warmth.

'They were the father and mother of them two dogs there,' he said.

On Christmas night it was so cold that he slept in a byre, warmed by the breath of the cattle. He told me he could recognize the 'tonguing' of his own dogs among the others as they hunted over the Cooley mountains on St Stephen's Day.

When he got home, the dogs ran ahead of him up the lane, but nobody came to the half-door to greet him. A neighbour woman was sitting in the kitchen. She told him that his brother was dead and buried.

'A stroke,' she said, 'we didn't know when you were coming home.'

He never hunted again.

'Why not?' I asked.

'Sure there was no one to tell it to,' he said to me, as he tied the bag of potatoes on the carrier of my bicycle, 'no one at all.'

And I watched him walking back up the lane, his two dogs close and warm by his side.

Three Cheers for the
Souls in Purgatory

Mickey was the greatest religious expert I ever knew, particularly knowledgeable on the subject of sin, and he was responsible for me having a profound religious experience when I was nine years of age. He was small, weedy, twelve years old, and he had the same fascination for me as a ferret has for a rabbit. He would deliver his judgements before school began in the mornings. When two boys went into the grounds of the Protestant church, he said that looking in through the window was a venial sin but going into the church was a mortal sin and needed to be told in confession. We all believed him.

One day, outside the chapel, he produced a box of matches. 'I wonder,' he said, 'could you crack a match on that cement.'

'Of course you could,' I said and rasped the match against the ground so that it burst into flame.

'That's a sin,' he said, 'because that's consecrated ground. It's called sacrilege. You'll have to tell it in confession.'

The parish priest had a habit of starting every sentence with the word 'but' and he was also slightly deaf. When I told him, he said, 'But what say?' and I repeated the sin.

'I struck a match on the chapel yard.'

'But do you smoke?' he asked.

'No, Father,' I replied.

'But that's no sin at all,' he said. 'Three Hail Marys.'

And then one day in school Mickey said to me, 'There's a dance in the Orange Hall tonight. Me and you will go up to find out what goes on there,' and he added, 'if you don't go I'll tell everyone you're a coward.'

I was afraid of my parents but I was more afraid of him and that night, I sneaked out of the bedroom window and met him at the hall. We hovered around, retreating into the darkness if anyone came out of the hall and advancing into the circle of light when they had gone back in. Then round the back we discovered a toilet window open high up on the wall. We climbed up and stood on a couple of the bicycles that were leaning against the gable. We could hear the MC.

'And now,' he said, 'three cheers for the ladies who

prepared the supper. Hip! Hip!' They were given. 'And three cheers for the band. Hip! Hip!'

Mickey said to me, 'We'll shout, "Three cheers for the souls in purgatory." I'll count to three. One, two, three,' and I yelled in through the toilet window, 'Three cheers for the souls in purgatory!'

But I yelled alone. He had melted into the darkness and there I was, standing on a bicycle saddle, silhouetted against the lighted window of the packed Orange Hall, late at night, at nine years of age, having just struck a blow for the faithful departed. I know now that nobody could have heard me but I jumped down and flew home, terrified of furious Orangemen behind me and my parents before me.

Next day in school Mickey said that I had committed the sin of blasphemy, and I would have to tell it in confession. That night in the chapel when it came my turn, I decided to get it over quickly.

I said, 'I committed the sin of blasphemy. I shouted "Three cheers for the souls in purgatory" in through the window of the Orange Hall.'

'But what say?' said the priest, and I had to repeat it louder. I knew that it echoed over the whole chapel. There was a long pause. I could make out his shape through the curtain and I was sure his shoulders were shaking.

At length he said, 'But were you by yourself?'

'No, Father.'

'But stay away from the Orange Hall – and from bad company. Three Hail Marys.'

Deaf people often don't realize how loud they talk, and so it was that after he had given me absolution, I distinctly heard him mutter to himself, 'But if that little pup Mickey sends anybody else in here with a cock and a bull story, but I'll . . .'

His words were cut off by the slamming of the shutter.

The Stations of the Cross

When my uncle in New York was old and wandering in his mind he kept asking to be taken to the Yellow River, a stream that flowed near his old home in a desolate part of North Leitrim, and when I heard this it reminded me of a story he had told me about another of my ancestors who came from there. He was my great-uncle, and he lived in a townland of poor mountainy ground with its own outlying chapel. It was a poor building but contained a beautiful set of Stations of the Cross which were the pride and joy of the parishioners. The figures stood out from the pictures in relief so that you felt you could reach out and touch the the suffering faces.

One Sunday the parish priest announced that Confirmation was to be held in the parish church, four miles away, in a prosperous district, and that in order to impress the bishop, he would take the loan of the stations and erect them in the main church during his visit. Nobody said anything against this. It was not lucky to cross the priest and this one was a fearsome man. The stations were removed.

Confirmation came and went but there was no sign of them being returned. Eventually someone plucked up the courage to ask him. They would stay, he said, in the parish church where they could be seen and not buried away far up the mountain at the back of Godspeed, and that, he said, was an end of the matter. The mountain people went to Mass and looked at the fourteen clean empty rectangles on the walls and raged silently at the injustice but were afraid to do anything.

One summer Sunday, my great-uncle took the pony and cart down to the Yellow River. He washed the cart inside and out. He even brushed the dirt from the inside of the wooden wheel spokes. He tilted it up with its long shafts in the air until it dried while he cleaned and polished the pony harness. Then he put a clean white sheet in the cart and headed down the road to the parish church. He backed the cart up to the door, spread the sheet over the floor and sides, went into the church and started lifting the sacred pictures one by one off the walls and loading them into the cart.

It was the housekeeper who saw him first. She rushed

to the parochial house. The parish priest exploded out of the door, fixing his biretta on his head, and tore down to the church, his soutane flapping about his legs. He was a big man and he was apoplectic with rage.

'How dare you? How dare you?' he shouted. 'You are desecrating the house of God. Put those back immediately.' He towered over my relation. 'It is my command and the command of his lordship the bishop of this diocese that they stay in this church.'

'Now listen, Father,' said my great-uncle in his quiet way, 'it was my people and their relations in America who paid their hard-earned money for those stations and priest or no priest, bishop or no bishop they are going back to where they belong. Now you're blocking the door, Father, and if you don't get out of my way there'll be more desecrated round here than the house of God.'

There was a menace in his soft voice and the holy man stood to one side.

The Yellow River still flows down near Killavoggy chapel. The houses of my uncle and great-uncle are ruined and empty now, inhabited only by their ghosts. But I like to think that occasionally they glide across and look in the chapel window and gaze on the Stations of the Cross, with figures you could almost touch, that they paid for with their hard-earned money, and smile about a day long ago when a small man with a pony walked to the parish church and returned a hero.

Hounds and Hares

He could spit further than any other person I ever knew. Once I saw him stand behind an ass and cart and spit right out over the ass's ears. On fair days he never came to school, and in the early morning I would sit in the window and watch for him driving cattle for some strong farmer up past our house, his ashplant nonchalantly over his shoulder. Once he pointed it at me and pretended to shoot me, blew imaginary smoke off the end of it, and then spat accurately on to the rump of one of the cows. I could never spit like him, though I practised assiduously in the garden until my father told me to stop. But it is another day which really stands out in my memory.

We lived close to the primary school and I used to go home every day for my lunch. I always hated it because

I knew that while I was away the big boys would be playing 'Hounds and Hares' and that I would be left out.

Invariably when I got back to school, teams had already been picked and they were away running like young colts, wild and free, over the bogs and fields behind the school, while I was left in the playground with the girls and the small boys, miserably scuffing the dusty ground with my foot. Not that I would have had much chance of being picked anyway, because I was two years younger than the rest of my class.

But when the master blew the whistle for the end of playtime, I would go in and sit in the long empty desk and await the return of the warriors, always a few minutes late, sweating and breathless.

All afternoon I would listen to whispered tales of the chase, of bare feet flying like the wind over the ground, of hares being captured and breaking free again, of zig-zag pursuits through the graveyard where you were caught if you stepped on a grave, of mighty deeds of valour performed when farmers had set their dogs on them. I heard and I longed with every fibre of my being to be part of it. I knew too that they always returned via the spring well where they would drink the water that was so cold it would give you a pain below your eyes.

It was dangerous to drink directly from the spring because a man-keeper, a newt, would go into your mouth and down your throat and the only way to get it back out again was to eat nothing but salt for seven days and then go back and hold your mouth open over the well and the man-keeper, crazed with thirst, would jump out and back into the water. This I knew to be nothing less than the biblical truth, the same as the fact that if you put a horse-hair across the palm of your hand when you were about to be slapped, the cane would split in two.

And then one day my parents had to go away and I was given lunch to eat in school. I was a bit ashamed of it because it consisted of sandwiches while the rest of the boys had oatcake, but to my surprise they were very anxious to swap and everything was satisfactory.

Then two of the biggest boys started picking teams, one group to be the hounds, the other the hares. The captain of the hounds was the boy who had shot me with his ashplant. Now I hovered around the edge of the circle as one boy after another was picked. Only the small boys were left and then the captain of the hounds pointed at me and said, 'You'. I was given one instruction. 'Stand in the chapel gate and don't let anyone past.' I would die first, I thought.

I stood between the stone pillars and watched the first group set off and then shortly afterwards the second. I listened to the distant shouting as each hare was caught and then it grew louder and louder as they came back. Suddenly a big lad came charging round the corner of the chapel heading for the gate, with the hounds some distance behind. He looked at the small figure in between the pillars and then over his shoulder. Clearly I was not worthy of his notice for he ran straight at me, not even bothering to dodge to one side. I leaped up and caught him with my two hands by the collar of his shirt. He swung me off my feet and shook me like a terrier with a rat.

'Get off me, you wee bastard,' he said, pushing the flat of his hand into my face. But I closed my eyes tight and held on. I could hear his shirt beginning to tear. He tried to run with me still hanging on to him, but it was no good and the hounds arrived. The big captain looked down at me and I looked up at him. Everybody looked at the two of us.

'God, you've got a grip like an owl,' he said. 'You're a great wee lad.' And he looked up at the spire and spat so high that I thought it would land on the chapel bell.

The Fourth Fall

He was a regular visitor to our house and I thought he had only one name, Tomeddy. But he really had two, Thomas Edward or Tom Eddy. He could make my parents laugh till the tears streamed down their faces. When a woman returned from New York, not having made good, he said that she got the roof of her mouth sunburnt looking up at the skyscrapers. My mother tut-tutted but my father thought it was hilarious. I couldn't understand it at all.

Now it was compulsory to attend the Stations of the Cross in the chapel during Lent when I was growing up. They always ended with the rosary being given out by a member of the congregation, a man noted for his extreme piety and for his respect for the clergy. This pious man modelled himself on the priests, even trying to walk like them. Tomeddy said he should have been one himself.

Then a new priest arrived, and we altar boys discovered two things, that he had a very short temper and that he had a funny way of saying the Hail Mary. Instead of 'Hail Mary full of grace,' he used to say, 'Tail Marry fullem grace.' Within a week, the pious man, when he was giving out the rosary, was saying, 'Tail Marry fullem grace.'

Tomeddy used to reply in a loud voice, 'Toly Marry motherem God.'

But the Stations of the Cross did not offer any opportunity for such levity. The priest, preceded by an altar boy carrying a candle, paused before each of the fourteen pictures of the Way of the Cross, and read out a meditation. I can still remember the lovely rolling phrases. 'Consider how those women wept with compassion at seeing Jesus in such a pitiable state, streaming with blood as he walked along. "My children," said he, "Weep not for me but for yourselves and for your children."' It could be very moving.

One evening I was carrying the candle. I was a very fidgety youngster and kept picking at the wax that flowed down the side of the candle. 'Stop it,' said the priest to me in between stations, but I continued when I thought he wasn't looking. Then we came to the tenth station, and he read, 'Consider the violence with which the executioners stripped Jesus. His inner garments adhered to his torn flesh, and they dragged them off so roughly that the skin came with them. Compassionate your Saviour thus cruelly treated.'

And with these words he gave me a tremendous box on the side of the head. I can still feel the cold of the flagstone of the aisle against my cheek as I lay on the ground and smell the plume of candle smoke rising from the glowing wick. There would be no more picking at the wax now because the candle was out. I got back up to my knees and the stations continued without a pause.

When we got back to the vestry the priest never said one word about the incident, but I knew I was in for trouble when I got home, for disgracing my parents in front of the whole parish. And I was right.

My father was waiting for me with a face like thunder. 'Come here you,' he said.

I looked appealingly at my mother but she was washing her hands at the kitchen sink and wanted nothing to do with this just man. I was for crucifixion. And then in walked Tomeddy. He had been at the chapel too.

'Well fair play to you, young fella,' he said when he saw me, 'we got good value tonight. There's usually only three falls in the stations, but tonight we got four.'

And thankfully, my parents laughed.

Killing the Pig

It was undoubtedly the most primitive house I had ever been in. The kitchen was dark and smoke-filled, the only light coming from the half-door and one small window covered in dirt and cobwebs. Hens walked freely over the concrete floor. There was a hearth fire with a crook for hanging the blackened cooking pots, a dresser with an array of Delft, every single one of which seemed to be cracked or chipped, and on an oil-cloth covered table there were mugs, plates, a jamjar half-full of milk, a canister containing tea and a paper bag of sugar.

'Sit down,' said the man of the house, 'I was just going to ate.'

I said that I wasn't hungry, but he would have none of it, because it was the convention in that part of the country that politeness would dictate that you would first of all refuse the offer of food. The correct phrase was, 'No, no, I'm only rising from the table.' But it was important that these formalities had to be gone through, and anyone who would take anything to eat in a neighbour's house without a little forcing would be considered forward, so there was nothing for it but to sit down at the table.

He lived alone and did his own cooking. On this particular day he announced proudly that he had made his own butter and produced a plate of the stuff from the dresser. There you are,' he said, 'I could churn with any woman.'

It was like nothing I had ever seen before, dark yellow in colour, with streaks of grey and black through it, and worst of all, hairs, whether animal or human I couldn't decide. I was picking through it with the knife trying to get a clean bit when he saw me. He reached over and then in the goodness of his heart, he said, 'Go on. Don't be shy, take a dacent bit of it.' And he plunged the knife into the butter and spread it thickly on my slice of bread.

He announced the programme for the day. 'I have to phone the vet,' he said. 'There's a calf with the scour. You have to help me with that, and we'll kill the pig in the afternoon. Come here till I show you.'

In one small shed, a calf was standing on a bed of

hay. The hay, the calf, the walls and the door were covered with liquid manure – the smell was frightful.

'The scour,' he said, 'it's a bad man.'

Nex, he went over to the pigsty, undid the rope that acted as a hinge, lifted away the slatted door and with great pride said, 'There she is.' He took off his hat and hit the pig on the rump to make it walk around.

I knew I was expected to make a comment, and I said, 'She looks well.'

He looked at me pityingly. 'She looks more than well,' he said, putting his hat back on, 'she's the best pig in the country. Get your bike.'

We headed down the road to the public telephone kiosk, or the 'kye sock' as he insisted on calling it. He didn't know how to use the phone, and I had to do the dialling. When I had put him through, he took the receiver and roared into it, 'Hello! Hello! This is Patterson's calf speaking!' And then in response to a question, 'Well, she's skitterin'away.'

I stood outside, holding the two bicycles in total embarrassment, hoping that none of my friends would come past, and watching the curtains of the post office twitch, as the postmistress, who listened in on all calls, looked out to check the identity of the caller.

'You'll be getting Jimmy this afternoon then,' I said on the way back to his house. Jimmy was the local expert butcher. He could get hold of one of the pig's ears with one hand, and hit it sharply with the wooden mallet on the head with the other. Down the pig would go, stunned, and immediately he would stab it with the knife, between the two forelegs, straight through the heart, and apart from a few twitches, it was dead.

'No indeed,' said the man, 'he's far too dear. There's a neighbour who'll do it just as well and for half the price.'

The neighbour was waiting when we got back, with a mallet tied to the bar of his bicycle. There was no greeting. He untied the mallet and then I saw that he also had an iron rod with a pointed hook on the end of it.

'It's a cleek,' he said to me, 'a cleek.'

He went into the sty, and I heard the pig squealing. He came out, leading the pig. He had stuck the cleek into the pig's mouth, and pushed the pointed hook out through its cheek. The animal couldn't move without tearing its cheek.

'Hold this,' he said.

I held the cleek, while the pig looked up at me, terrified. The man of the house held on to the rear of the animal to steady it, and the butcher hit it on the head with the mallet. The pig squealed but did not fall. He hit it again and yet again. The pig looked up at me and shrieked. I wanted to run. On and on it went. Eventually, out of sheer exhaustion from the blows, the pig sank to the ground, still screeching, till I thought it would curdle my blood. He got out a long knife, and pushing the animal over on its side, went down on one knee, lifted one of the forelegs, and stuck the knife in. Nothing happened except for a horrendous shriek from the pig.

He looked up at me, moving the knife around inside, and said, 'I can't find the heart.'

Suddenly there was a gush of dark red blood which flowed over the stones of the yard and over the abandoned cleek. 'Ah, that's better,' he said with great satisfaction.

The pig's eyes closed, the squealing died away, it kicked a few times and then it was still.

'We'll scald it and shave it,' said the butcher, 'and then we'll hang it on the ladder and we'll open its waistcoat.'

But at that stage, I could take no more. I made my excuses, leapt on my bicycle and tore down the road home. My father said nothing when I told him, just muttered something about growing up, and told me to weed the onions. But that night and for many nights after, my sleep was filled with nightmares of tortured animals and agonized screams, horrific smells and being forced under pain of death to eat the most loathsome food imaginable.

The Rabbit Island

Nobody lives on the Rabbit Island any more. Nobody swims at the Sand-bed. It is too dangerous. The bottom is littered with cans and broken bottles, and even syringes. But when I was growing up it was the place to be on a summer Sunday. There was a long hill on the road down to it and you could free-wheel the last mile with the swimming togs wrapped in the towel on the carrier at the back of the bike.

In those days there were no such things as armbands or floats when you were learning to swim. You went up to the back of the local pub, collected corks from the porter bottles, tied them securely in a flour bag and trusted that they would keep you afloat. The more sophisticated among us used the inflated rubber inner-tube from a lorry wheel. Or you simply cut and tied a sheaf of rushes, and lay across them as they floated on the water. All practising was done privately in the icy brown waters of one of the local rivers and only when you could swim a few strokes unaided would you consider that you had graduated to the dizzy heights of public display.

Only boys went swimming at the Sand-bed. The girls sat on the grass in their summer dresses and watched. The boys would tog out at a respectable distance and then would all gallop down to the water leaping over thistles and clumps of nettles on the way and the brave ones would hurl themselves bodily into the water while the timid ones like myself would inch their way into the deeper water, hands gripped together, body curved inward, flinching as the cold water crept up our bodies.

Nobody had swimming trunks in those days, everybody wore football togs. These were figure-hugging when they got wet. Worse still, white ones became transparent. I have seen boys coming out of the water backways in embarrassment and one lad spent two and a half mortal hours in the water, coming out when the girls had gone away, his skin wrinkled like a prune.

Always after a while splashing about, half a dozen of the big lads would set off to swim to the Rabbit Island, about half a mile away. I watched enviously as they went, chatting nonchalantly to each other, and some time later

I could see their distant figures strolling casually about the shoreline of the island. I knew that they were the focus of all eyes and that when they came out, they would dry themselves and come over and sit beside the girls, hair still wet, glowing with achievement. It became my ambition to swim to the island, and I fixed the date for a Sunday when all the big fellows would be away at a football match and I would have all the attention to myself. I could swim all of twenty yards with a sort of labour-intensive breast stroke, but in my vanity this minor point was completely overlooked.

At first all went well. I seemed to be making good progress and I could imagine the admiring glances from the shore, but gradually I tired and realized that the island was much further away than I had thought. I had now reached the point where I had to decide whether to go on or go back, what World War One pilots used to call the point of no return. It was a contest between pride and fear, and pride won. There was an expanse of reeds that stuck out a hundred yards from the island and I headed for these. The water was still deep but I could rest by catching on to a clump of the reeds which supported me.

Only then did it dawn on me that I would have to swim back. I was dog-tired and starting to shiver with the cold. I could, of course, shout for help, or go round the hundred yards to the island and ask the woman there to row me across in her boat, but that would be too shame-making.

Taking a deep breath I started back. As I became more and more tired my legs sank lower and lower in the water which slowed down my progress even more. The clouds came and covered the sun, the heat went out of the day and a cold breeze ruffled the surface of the lake and blew grey waves into my mouth. I could see the crowds leaving. Stories of people getting cramp, of giant pike which would take your leg off and eels that would coil around your limbs came to mind. I thought of my old schoolmaster who was fond of saying, 'The paths of glory lead but to the grave,' and I could almost hear the words at the funeral – 'Taken from us before the promise of his young life was fulfilled.' I struggled feebly on. I was about halfway and near total exhaustion when a miracle happened. My feet touched bottom, a small underwater mound that I did not know existed. I stood there, chest-deep, panting and nearly crying with relief. When I got my breath back, I set off again, knowing I would make it safely.

I came ashore, my fingers and toes numb and corpse-white. I was shuddering so violently that it took me ages to dress. My bicycle was the only one left. Somebody had let the air out of the tyres. It was the final ignominy, the paths of glory did really lead nowhere, my day of triumph had turned to ashes and dust, but I was past caring and started to walk home, pushing the bike bumpily up the long steep hill.

An Inspector Calls

In the Forties and Fifties, the two figures who struck terror into the hearts of principals of small country schools were the school inspector and the parish priest, but principals had their own ways of coping. One inspector's report of the time states, 'The children were unresponsive to even the simplest questions. When I asked the principal for an explanation, he said, "This is poteen-making country and from an early age the children are taught not to answer any questions from strangers."'

More spectacular was the method employed by one principal whose pupils were still out playing at two-thirty on a summer afternoon, when he spotted the inspector's car coming up the road. A deep river flowed around the playground and the principal was a strong swimmer.

With commendable quickness of thought he flung one of the boys into the river, and as the car drove in the gate, the inspector beheld the sight of the principal diving into the river and rescuing a drowning pupil. He even got a commendation from the Department of Education!

I personally knew the principal of one local school, who was famed for her dedication and industry. She used to take the children back to school in the evenings for extra lessons, and even taught on Saturday mornings. She was known to stop on her high bicycle at a hayfield and order the children out of it and into school. The three R's and the catechism were the staple diet and she regarded such fripperies as music as a waste of time. There was one Protestant pupil at the school who used to be sent out to the porch during religious lessons. One day the new parish priest came on visitation.

'What are you doing?' he said to the boy.

'I'm tidying the turf,' said he.

'Bless yourself,' said the priest.

He did so.

'Say the Confiteor.'

He was word-perfect.

'Name the sorrowful mysteries.'

He knew them.

The parish priest went into the classroom and told the principal that the boy had a first-class knowledge of his faith and as a reward he would give him a prize. He reached into his pocket and handed him a pair of rosary beads – and the principal never said a word!

Now the local inspector was a most unpleasant character who delighted in catching teachers out. One morning he arrived unexpectedly at the school and announced that he would spend the day conducting an examination in every aspect of schoolwork. He could find nothing wrong. The rolls were immaculately kept, arithmetic was perfect, creative English was excellent, the pupils read fluently, geography was satisfactory.

Towards the end of the day he turned to the principal; 'What about singing?' he said.

'Pardon?' she said.

'Singing.'

'Singing?'

'Yes, singing.'

'Oh very well,' she said, and turning to the class, 'Now children, fold your arms, sit up straight and pay attention. The inspector is going to sing for us.'

The White Horse

Obviously I was equivalent to one third of a horse. You see, we used to cut our own turf in the bog, a useful way of saving money on fuel in the late Forties. The only problem was that we had no horse to bring the turf home when it was saved, and so I would be hired out for three days to a farmer and then we would get the loan of his horse for one day. This led to me working in many strange places.

One of them was a small mountainy farm that was situated, as they say, at the back of Godspeed. When I asked a friend of mine where it was, he said, 'You've heard of the back of beyond, well it's behind that again.'

A middle-aged childless couple lived there. He had the rolling gait and powerful shoulders of a man used to heavy manual work. He always wore a cap, and spoke very little. She was known as being slightly odd, and she seemed slightly embarrassed at having a schoolboy working for them. But I never minded, because they were kindness personified, and as well as that, their horse was the finest animal in the country.

It was white, with a long flowing mane that had never been trimmed, about seventeen hands high, gentle and obedient, and easy to handle, even for a novice like myself. It had one brown eye and one blue eye and when it turned its head and looked at you, I often thought it was like one of those pictures whose eyes seemed to follow you approvingly, no matter where in the room you were.

When we went out into the field to catch it, it would come voluntarily. The man always brought a stool for me to stand on, while I reached up and put on the headstall and slipped the bit into the horse's mouth, and the huge animal stood patiently putting up with my clumsy efforts. I had to run to keep up with its enormous strides.

Under the farmer's benevolent eye, I quickly learned how to put on its harness, ducking under its body to fasten the various leather straps and tightening them as I had seen him do. He rarely said anything, just shook his head or nodded it. But more than anything else, I wanted to be able to do it correctly so that I could tell the boys in school that I had harnessed a horse to a cart. I had already learned a number of important skills, like how to wheel a barrow by pulling it behind you by the shafts instead of pushing it in front of you, or being able to get on a man's bicycle by throwing my leg over the saddle instead of under the bar. And I felt that this was another vital stage in my education.

I used to lie in bed at night thinking about it, and name the various pieces of harness in my mind in case I would forget them, the straddle, the britchen, the collar and the hames, the headstall and the bit.

Although he never said so, it was clear that this big, quiet man was proud of the animal and occasionally he would slap it on the rump with his hand, or stroke its neck and grunt approvingly.

One day he said to me, 'There's never any need to bate a good horse.'

Another day he said, 'I broke it in myself.'

And another time, 'Horses get like the people that own them.'

And sometimes, oh joy of joys, I would have to bring it to the forge to get shod, riding bareback down the road, able to see over tall hedges into the fields, and praying that I would meet some of my schoolfriends, so that I could casually pull on the reins and say 'Woa there, woa there,' to my steed, and sit sideways on his broad back as I talked from on high, and pretend that I wasn't swelling with pride, that this was the most natural thing in the world, all in a day's work to me.

I remember once singing a song I had heard from my mother, 'Cruising Down the River on a Sunday Afternoon', and then changing the words to 'Going for the Horseshoes on a Tuesday Afternoon', and thinking that I was the wittiest person in the whole of the entire universe. And at other times I could imagine myself as one of the legendary warriors of old, charging out of the mists from their halls inside the mountain into battle, and my back would straighten and my small chest expand and I whirled the reins about my head as I rode this great lumbering carthorse to the forge. There have been just a few times in my young life when I could say that I have been supremely happy, and riding the big white horse down the road of my childhood was one of them. But it was not to last.

Some weeks later, my father came in with the news that he had been asked to phone the vet, because the white horse was badly injured. He had tried to jump a barbed-wire fence, and one of the posts had gone deeply into his stomach. The vet could do nothing. My father said that as it lay on the ground, it suddenly kicked violently and died.

I went up to see the man a few days later. I said I was sorry to hear about his horse. Strangely, he was talkative.

'Did the lorry come to take him away?' I asked.

'I buried him,' he said. 'Myself and a neighbour dug a hole five feet deep and six feet long, got a pony and we dragged him with chains to the edge. Then I got an axe and cut off the legs and the head and pushed the whole lot into the hole. We covered him with blackthorns to keep the dogs and foxes away, and filled it in.'

All this he told me quite matter-of-factly and I was shocked. But I should have realized that my feelings were the sentimentalities of a tourist. I should also have stopped talking, but I blundered on.

'You must be sorry after it,' I said.

There was a pause.

'Don't mention it to herself inside,' he said, and he walked into the turfhouse past the harness hanging from hooks in the wall – the straddle, the britchen, the collar and the hames, the headstall and the bit.

Lords of the Dance

The AOH was the first hall in our area where dances were held. The letters stood for Ancient Order of Hibernians, though the boys in school told me that they stood for All Ould Hoors. I believed them, though I didn't understand the meaning at the time, and it confused my spelling for years afterwards. Ours was the only part of the country where the word 'Hoor' could be interpreted as a compliment. 'He's a hoor of a worker,' people would say approvingly, or, 'He's a hoor to mark,' of a good footballer.

An older friend of mine told me about the dances. There was no electricity in the area, so lighting was supplied by the ubiquitous Tilley lamps which needed constant pumping to keep up the paraffin vapour pressure.

Eight of them were hung up, hissing, on the walls. Before the dance started, men went round with buckets, sprinkling water and disinfectant on the floor to keep down the dust, so that the whole place smelt of antiseptic. My friend told me that to this day, he can never smell Jeyes Fluid without recalling his dancing days, and he laughed as he described them to me.

The MC made his announcements through a megaphone, which looked for all the world like a conical coal scuttle with no bottom. He had a habit of announcing everything in one sentence.

'Choose your partners for an old-time waltz Johnny Maguire pump the Tilleys,' or, 'There are three bicycles causing an obstruction at the gate please remove them immediately the next dance will be a quickstep.'

It was a great thing to have a bicycle in those days and one man used to dance with the bicycle clips visible in the top pocket of his jacket so that his partner could see that if everything worked out, she had a lift home on the bar.

There seemed to be no fixed number in the band. One night there might be three on stage and on another, there would be, as my friend described it, 'A forest of fiddles.' One man, a great fiddler, could fill the hall all by himself. Apparently he used to hang another fiddle on the back wall, and it would pick up the sympathetic vibrations from his own playing, and act as an amplifier.

On one occasion, as often happened, a man was called on for a song. He was a member of the church choir and to everyone's astonishment, he sang, '*I'll sing a hymn to Mary, the mother of my God, The virgin of all virgins of David's royal blood . . .*' Out of respect, everybody listened and at the end there was a spattering of applause.

Then a voice from the back shouted up, 'And there'll be Benediction after the next dance.'

Sometimes in the crowded hall, disputes would break out, over politics, or ancient family feuds, or football, or land, or more rarely, a girl. When a man was going to fight he took off his coat, and then his waistcoat and then turned his cap back to front. The threats from these warriors to opponents were fearsome in the extreme.

'I'll toss you where you stand.'

'Don't bother taking off that coat, I'll bate it off you.'

'I often knocked better men than you out of me way to get at a good man.'

'I'll whitewash the ground with your blood.'

'Hould me back before I kill him.'

And sometimes from a champion who regretted his challenge; 'Is there no one to hould me back? I'll not fight if there's no one to hould me back.' In fact one man earned the nickname, 'Let me at him hould me back'.

Usually all this bluster was just that, the mock-battle posturings of two young bulls vying for territory, and frequently things were settled before any actual physical violence occurred. But sometimes they became very serious indeed.

There was one particular incident when a young blood, home on holiday from England and spoiling for a fight, decided to pick on a big, quiet, inoffensive man who was present at the dance. He pushed him, bumped into him deliberately, called him names. The big man stood there for a long time impassively, like a quiet ox, no movement except for a pulse beating visibly in his neck, refusing to be provoked. The younger man joined a group of his friends and they all laughed loudly, looking over at the victim.

They must have mistaken the awful pallor of the big man's face for fear, instead of what it was, murderous rage. Suddenly he walked deliberately out into the middle of the floor where his tormentor was standing. He pushed two of the group aside as if they were chaff, caught him by the throat with his two hands, and lifting him off the ground shook him like a terrier with a rat. The younger man wriggled free and ran out the door of the hall, pursued by the big man. He leaped on a bicycle to escape, and his pursuer leaped on another. The chase lasted for twenty miles till they came to the town of Cavan where the hunted man escaped in a maze of streets.

The young man later spoke of the terror of that night. He said that the worst part was the silence. There were no shouts or threats, but every time he looked around, there was the huge shape of the big man on the bicycle coming remorselessly after him on the moonlit road.

'I could feel the breath of death behind me,' he said.

A couple of days later, he left for England, never to return. And for him, just as well.

Years afterwards, I asked the big man, with whom I was now friendly, about the incident.

'What would you have done if you had caught him?'

'I would have killed him,' he said quietly.

'Killed him?' I asked.

'Yes, killed him,' he said, 'I'm an old man now, and I still would. He was only a hoor's melt.'

And this time it most certainly was not a compliment.

Gorman's Reel

In the Forties John was the up-and-coming young fiddler in our area. His musical ear was as good as a tape-recorder. Play a tune for him once and he had it off. With his thick black wavy hair and his handsome sallow face, he was much in demand to play at the local country house dances. He could not read a note of music. There was no need to when he could learn every reel, jig or hornpipe by just listening to someone playing them, and the local fiddlers all played by ear. All, except for one.

Old Bartley Duggan lived far down the bog pass on the shores of Upper Lough Erne. In wintertime the lough rose and surrounded his small thatched house on its hump of ground, so that it was perched on a tiny island and he had to go and come by boat. And in wintertime too, you would see his light burning far into the night and people would say, 'Bartley is at the notes again.'

And so he would be, poring over a yellowing manuscript, wire-rimmed glasses close to the page, slowly and painfully trying over each phrase on his fiddle. Or sitting at the corner of the kitchen table, the dishes from his previous meal shoved to one side, laboriously copying out a magpie-like collection of tunes acquired over the years. Hour after hour he would sit there alone. No sound but the scrape of his pen, the tick of the clock, the water at the door. Yes, Bartley Duggan had the notes and he regarded all others as his inferiors.

One day John and he met on the road. 'Well, young fellow,' he said in his big voice that you could hear three townlands away. 'Well, young fellow, they tell me you play the fiddle.'

'I do,' said John.

'Can you read the notes?' asked Bartley.

'No, I can't.'

'Aha!' he boomed. 'You can play none so.'

Worse was to follow, for shortly after this, John's uncle in America sent him a new reel, written in notes on music manuscript. 'It's called "Gorman's Reel",' said the covering letter, 'it's a good one, and I'm looking forward to hearing you play it when I'm home in the summer.' John had to bring it to Bartley and ask him if he would learn it and then teach it to him.

A week passed. Bartley hadn't time to look at it, he said. Another week passed and then another. When John called at the house there was no answer although the dog was at the door. Sometimes he would see Bartley down the pass, or at a gap in the hedge, or over in the bog, but when he got there he would have disappeared, like the will-o'-the-wisp that people said wandered the bog at night. It was clear the tune was not coming back.

One day John was setting potatoes in a field just inside the thick whitethorn hedge which bordered the bog pass when he heard old Bartley coming whistling. Now John knew all of Bartley's tunes but this was a new one. He quietly put down the spade and as Bartley walked up the pass he kept pace with him unseen on the inside of the hedge, listening. By the time they reached the end of the hedge John had the tune. He dashed home, got out his fiddle and played it over to make sure he remembered it. Then he put his fiddle under his coat and headed off for Bartley's house.

'Here's a new reel I learned, Bartley,' he said. 'Did you ever hear it?'

And he stood in the kitchen and played 'Gorman's Reel'.

'Where did you hear that one?' Bartley demanded.

'I got it off you,' replied John, 'when you were whistling it up the bog pass.'

117

'Well bad luck to you for a yellow bastard,' Bartley boomed venomously. 'It's not safe for a man to open his mouth round the bogs any more. I'll quit playing.'

The Fiddle Maker

The violin was my favourite instrument, at once the most difficult and the most rewarding. I was fortunate to have had a natural aptitude for the instrument and to have been blessed with good teachers. My favourite was an elderly nun, equally renowned for her wonderful examination results, and for her sharp temper. Lessons took place in a room called St Joseph's Parlour, with windows of frosted glass opening on to a corridor leading to the convent chapel. Sometimes as I waited for my lesson, I could see through the glass the ghostly figures of the sisters as they processed, chanting, into prayer. It scared the wits out of me, and I never knew if I should be practising or not, because it seemed vaguely sacrilegious. Then in would come my teacher and tell me that I was idling, or else that I was playing badly.

I remember on one occasion, she asked me to come up to the convent when she was taking another young lad for a violin lesson. The idea, I suppose, was that he would hear me play, and thus be encouraged, or, as I thought, inspired. She always held a violin and bow in her hands, and frequently, she would beat time with the bow. 'Listen,' she said to the young lad, 'Start,' she said to me, and blithely, I did so, showing off, lacking in concentration and full of the pride that goes before a fall. I had played just a few bars when she suddenly gave me a tremendous rap across the knuckles with the bow. 'Play it properly,' she said. 'Start again.' And I did, playing much better, with bruised and stinging fingers. She nodded grimly. 'That's better,' she said. 'You see,' she said to my fellow sufferer. 'It's not difficult when you concentrate.'

For some reason, I really liked that nun. She was never motivated by malice, simply by a love of music and the desire to get her pupils to play to their full potential. The other lad never came back.

Later, when I went to university, I took lessons from a lady who was leader of the Ulster Orchestra. She was a fearsome, big-bosomed woman. One day she was talking about my bow arm not being supple enough. She grasped my arm to show me how it should be moving. Then she stopped. 'Roll up your sleeve,' she said. She looked at my arm in disgust. 'Where did you get those muscles?' she said. 'What sport do you do?'

'Rowing,' I said.

'There's only one thing worse for a violinist than rowing,' she said, 'That's tennis. Although,' she added, 'You're not as bad as another of my pupils. He has a marvellous ear, but he has the biggest arms I have ever seen. Guess what his occupation is.'

'A builder,' I said.

'He's a pastry cook,' she said. 'He got the muscles kneading the dough.'

Now most musicians in our community played by ear but there was always great respect for someone who had 'the notes', and so it was that I gained a reputation for musical knowledge. One day, a man came to our door. He was small, neat and polite. Rather shyly he told me that he had made a fiddle, and would I be able to come to his house to test it out, since he had heard that I was an expert. Modestly I disclaimed any such title but I said I would be delighted to come, and made an appointment for a few days time. I knew nothing about the making of fiddles, so in order to preserve my reputation, I visited the library and read a book about the great violin makers of Cremona, especially Stradivarius and Guarnerius. In the book was a pull-out section which contained a full-scale drawing of one of Stradivarius' violins. I absorbed as much information as I could, and left the library, confident that I would live up to the fiddlemaker's expectations of me.

On the day of the visit, I followed the directions he had given me; down a narrow gravel road over the bog, careful because there is a drop down on each side, take the second lane on the left, the house is in front of you.

And so it was. A small slate-roofed house, which had obviously once been a thatched cottage, with a cobbled area in front. It had its own shelter belt of clipped whitethorn hedges, so that as I got out of the car I could almost feel the stillness of the air and in the quietness, hear the hum of bees in the neat flowerbeds.

And there he was, standing in the doorway, smiling a welcome. He had dressed for my visit, in suit, collar and tie, and he greeted me in a courtly country way.

'You're welcome there,' he said, shaking hands with me. 'This is your first time, and I hope it won't be the last.'

Through the whitethorn hedges, Lough Erne gleamed in the summer sunlight, and I thought that the scene could have come straight out of a child's picture book. 'That's the Lough,' I said, rather stupidly.

'It is,' he said. 'That's the Lough all right.'

'Have you a boat?' I asked.

'I used to have, but I gave it away. Too much bother

looking after the wooden ones, and I don't like the fibreglass,' he said.

'I'm sure that on a hot day like this you could cool off with a swim in the Lough,' I said.

He laughed. 'Not at all,' he said. 'Sure I can't swim. Nobody living round the Lough can swim.'

There was a large, old-fashioned rose bush growing near the door. It was covered in the most wonderful cream-coloured blooms and as I got nearer, the air was heavy with its scent. I couldn't take my eyes off it and I stood still.

'You like the rose,' he said, obviously pleased. 'My grandmother brought it with her when she got married and came to this house. She was reared on one of the islands out there. That rose was her mother's before her. It's a way of remembering them all, I suppose.'

His wife had died years before. There were no children and he lived alone. 'Come in. Come in,' he said.

The kitchen was immaculate and he had the kettle already boiling on the cooker, and cups and saucers on the table. I said over tea that I had heard that he had been a great footballer, and he said that he had been, 'Handy enough'. Delicately, he waited for me to bring up the subject of the fiddle.

'How on earth do you set about making a fiddle?' I asked. 'You must have very sophisticated tools.'

He took a wooden box from under the table. 'There

they are,' he said. He had made them all himself: a special chisel from the point of the blade of an old scythe, the steel tempered by years of sharpening; a gauge for measuring the thickness of the back and the belly of the violin; animal glue that had to be boiled over the fire. He talked about wood, how it had to be seasoned, the resonating qualities of the different types, hardwood for the back, softwood for the belly, the proper grain and age of the timber, the correct positioning of a soundpost. I listened, awestruck, to this little man, whose craft was in direct lineal descent from the great violin makers of Europe. He had been born in the wrong century, I thought.

He went up to the other room and brought down a wooden violin case. It was beautifully made, wide at one end, and with just the right amount of taper towards the other. He opened it and there was the fiddle. The case was padded inside with semi-circular protuberances of cloth-covered polystyrene to match the shape of the instrument, so that when he took it out, the exact shape was left behind, like a sculptor's empty mould for a statue. He held the fiddle gently, stroking its curves as if it were a baby. Then he handed it to me, holding both hands underneath as if I were a knight being presented with a sword. It was almost like a liturgy, I thought. Even to the scent of the rose wafting through the open door like a beautiful incense. The violin was unexpectedly flawless, and I gasped.

'She's not tuned up,' he said. 'Don't be afraid to tighten the strings. Here's a bow, try it out.' The tone was hard, but true. 'She needs playing,' he said.

'Correct,' I replied, 'and anyway I can't do it justice because I'm not used to it.' I tried another few runs on it, and already, the tone seemed to improve. It was no Stradivarius, but it certainly was a beautiful instrument.

'Just a minute,' he said. He went back up to the room, and lo and behold, arrived down with another violin. 'Try that one,' he said. 'Which one is the best?' he asked when I had done so.

'Well both of them are lovely instruments,' I said diplomatically.

'One of them must be better,' he said. 'Which one?'

'Do you know?' I asked.

'I think I do,' he said

'Well, I think, perhaps the first one,' I replied.

'You're right,' he said.

And I felt ridiculously pleased. 'How did you know?' I asked. 'Did you try them out yourself?'

'Me? Not at all,' he laughed. 'Sure I'm tone deaf. I can't play anything. I can't even sing in tune. I just knew by the feel of them.' And he carefully packed away the instruments in their cases.

I decided that it was time for me to impress him with my knowledge. 'There's a book in the library,' I said,

'And there's a pull-out section showing a full-size drawing of one of Stradivarius' violins.'

He went over to a chest of drawers, long flat drawers of the type used by architects, took out and unrolled a large sheet of paper, and there it was, an exact copy of the drawing which he had painstakingly copied out in pencil at the library, and inked in when he got home. 'Would that be it?' he asked with a slight twinkle. 'That first violin has exactly those measurements. Though indeed it's no Strad.'

I had one shot left in my locker. 'Did you ever hear, Gerry, of a crane's leg being used for the soundpost?' And I swear, he went to another drawer and showed me six crane's legs. He took one out.

'That leg,' he said, 'is a masterpiece of engineering. See, it's hollow to make it light, and there are zig-zag struts of bone inside for strength because the crane is a big bird.' I humbly accepted this lesson in physics. 'You never said anything about the bow,' he said.

'It's horsehair. I had it in the house for years and it cost me a desperate hammering from my father when I was growing up. There was a man came one night, a neighbour, for a visit. He came in a pony and cart. I had an old bow that needed re-hairing and I sneaked out and cut half the tail off the pony. It did no harm, it was going to grow again and I thought they wouldn't notice it, but they did. Boy did I suffer,' he laughed. 'The proper hair

is camel hair, but there's not many camels around here
. . . Though there's plenty of people with humps on them.'
And we both collapsed in laughter.

After a while, I got up to go. 'Hold on for a minute,'
he said, and went back up to the room one more time.
When he came down, he was carrying a harp, an Irish
harp, not the big orchestral one.

'No,' I said 'You didn't make that.'

'Nobody else,' he said.

The frame was carved of beautiful mahogany, old
wood that he had bought years ago at an auction in a
Big House. On the curved side, he had carved a serpent
that looked as if it were alive and crawling up the
instrument. On the post he had inlaid ivy leaves. It was
fully strung.

'Gerry,' I said, 'I know nothing about harps but that
is a masterpiece. Why don't you put it on exhibition?
I could get someone who knows to come and look at
it.'

'No, no,' he said, 'It's only a hobby with me. I'm glad
you liked the instruments. You'll be back. I'm going to
make a guitar. I've decided to go modern.' And he laughed
again.

We shook hands and parted. It had been an extra-
ordinary, almost surreal experience. I drove out between
the whitethorn hedges with the lake shining through
them, over the gravelled bog road, and I thought about

how crass I had been to think that my superficiality could even begin to compare with his gentle wisdom, his wonderful skill, and his store of knowledge and affection for his craft. I smiled wryly to myself when I thought of how he had structured the visit, almost like a play: first, the production of an extra fiddle, then keeping the big dramatic surprise of the harp until last.

I never did go back, but I visited him in hospital where he had been taken when suddenly he had been diagnosed with 'the bad thing.' He was distressed when he saw me and he started to cry.

The man in the next bed said, 'Now Gerry there's no use in that. You'll just have to face up to it.'

'I can't,' he said, looking small and frightened. I could not think of one word to say.

At his wake, the kitchen was full of people, relations and neighbours. But there was nobody up in the room from where he had brought his treasures for me to look at, and where he now lay, pale in his coffin, his marvellous craftsman's hands cold to my touch and still for ever.

All that is many years ago. I heard that the house has been bulldozed to turn it into a lakeside guesthouse. The instruments, the handmade tools have disappeared; the scented rose is buried under rubble. The whitethorn hedges have been uprooted, and nothing remains to mark the dwelling of a sensitive man who didn't know that he had the soul of a poet and the skill of an artist.

Donkeys

They reminded me of a caravan of camels as they walked meekly, nose to tail, under police escort up the lane to the barracks in the mists of the early morning. Except these were not camels, they were donkeys and they were not carrying spices or exotic Eastern cargo, but bags of artificial fertilizer, sulphate of ammonia. They were innocent prisoners of war, their owners, the smugglers, having disappeared into the darkness of the previous night.

In the Fifties there was a thriving smuggling industry along the border. Sulphate of ammonia could be bought for ten shillings per bag in the North, taken across the mountain by donkey and creel at night, and sold for three pounds in the South. Responsible for trying to prevent the smuggling were the local police, and my father was the sergeant in charge.

At school my classmates saw no contradiction in the fact that their fathers were smugglers while mine was doing his best to catch them. Only occasionally, groups of the bigger lads would talk seriously and secretly in a corner of the playground and all conversation would cease when I arrived, and myself and little Francie from the mountain would stand to one side. He was thin and timid and he reminded me of a frightened hare I had once seen, crouched on the ground, with great brown eyes and long ears flat back against its head. I could never get him to talk. When he came into school each morning he would glance round warily before sitting down. He never responded to teasing or bullying and eventually he was left alone.

That morning when I saw all the asses being housed in the outbuildings near the barracks, I asked my father if the boys could come over and ride them, and he said yes. So did the master. I was delighted, because this would win for me the respect of the big lads. In the afternoon we all trooped over to the barracks and under the benevolent eye of the two adults the asses were released.

The big lads had cut sticks out of the hedge and some of them had found bits of rope that they fashioned into crude reins. These heroes selected the liveliest and friskiest of the asses to ride. They galloped them across the lawn, jumped them over drains, raced each other, belabouring the animals unmercifully if they hesitated. Some of them could stand on the asses' backs at full gallop or vault on to their backs from behind. They yelled the names of their cowboy heroes; 'Look boys, Roy Rogers!' or 'Here comes Gene Autry!' and they used the heels of their bare feet as these filmstars used their spurs.

Occasionally one of them was thrown off as his mount kicked up its heels and he would be mocked and laughed at as he lay breathless on the ground. 'Hey gringo!' they would shout, in a ghastly Mexican accent. 'You should learn to ride, no?' and off they would gallop yelling, 'Adios amigo.'

I was left with a wise old grey donkey who refused to go faster than a walk, and headed every time for the orchard where the low-lying branches swept me off his back. Little Francie stood there watching with his troubled brown eyes.

Eventually the master blew the whistle, the asses were rehoused and we trooped back to school, sweating, excited, recounting mighty deeds of assmanship. My popularity, I was convinced, was assured. And then suddenly little Francie hurled himself at the biggest of the big lads.

'You had no right batin' our ass,' he shouted, flailing away with futile fists. 'You had no right batin' our ass,' he yelled again, crying bitterly.

The big lad held him effortlessly at arm's length. There was some laughter, but it was of the embarrassed kind. Everybody now knew the identity of at least one of the asses. We also were dimly aware of what had given Francie the courage to attack the big lad. Somehow the happiness of the afternoon seeped away and we walked silently into school, and looking at Francie's tearstained face at the end of the long desk I felt miserable and guilty.

A Policeman's Lot

My father never talked about his work until he retired and it was only then that I began to hear stories about his policing methods when he was in charge of a barracks in South Fermanagh during the Forties. Because of its remoteness and isolation, it was regarded by the police as a punishment station. If a policeman was incompetent or misbehaved in one of the larger stations, he was liable to be sent to South Fermanagh, which was the equivalent of being exiled to Siberia. The result was that my father had at least one deviant policeman to deal with, and this posed its own problems.

Once, he took a case against a man for making poteen and seized a bottle of the stuff as evidence. He kept it for safe-keeping in the cell which housed prisoners and the night before the case was to come up in court he went to check that it was still there. Unfortunately the resident alcoholic policeman had discovered it and the bottle was empty. This was serious – no evidence, no case, reprimand from the authorities. My father went up to the house of a well-known poteen maker.

'Tell me, Tommy,' he said, 'do you know where a man would get a drop of poteen?'

'Is it for yourself, Sergeant?'

'It is.'

'Well do you know, I might be able to lay hands on a drop if you call back in half an hour.'

Half an hour later, he had a full bottle in his possession, produced it in court next day, the judge sniffed it, said it was good stuff, the court dutifully laughed, my father asked for leniency, the fine was half-a-crown, the defendant paid and everyone was happy.

Every Sunday there was Church Parade when the men would march down to the main road and then were dismissed to go to their various church services. In the barracks was a man who had been demoted for misconduct from sergeant to constable. One Sunday he was missing from Church Parade and the other men told my father that he had said that according to King's Regulations, he did not have to get up on a Sunday morning to go to Mass. My father believed in direct action. He went up to the barracks, into the room where the man was snoring, lifted the bed by the end, man and all, and toppled him out, ordered him to dress in full uniform and marched him over to the chapel. After Mass he brought him round to the sacristy and introduced him to the parish priest and said that this man was most anxious to be involved in parochial work of all kinds!

But sometimes his methods did not have the expected result. At one stage there was a young policeman who was there because of his extreme gullibility. He was English and naïve as only the English can be in Ireland. One night he and my father seized a huge number of smuggled pigs. They housed them in a walled yard adjacent to a house, and the young Englishman was left in charge while my father went off to get a transport lorry to convey the pigs to the sheds at the barracks. While he was away, a young girl came out of the house.

'Now isn't he the hard man,' she said, 'leaving you outside there on a freezing cold night like this. Sure come on in man, dear, and take a cup of tea, the pigs will mind themselves.'

She was very pretty. He went inside and she gave him sandwiches and hot tea and cake and fluttered her eyelashes at him till he was dizzy. When he went back out, the pigs were gone. My father arriving with the transport lorry met the young constable driving a solitary pig down the road. It was lame and couldn't run off with the rest.

But of all the stories I heard him tell, I'll never forget my father describing the scene in court when a totally stupid constable prosecuted a motorist for careless driving. The motorist had crashed at night into a cow which was standing on the road in the dip between two hills. The constable was being cross-examined by the solicitor for the defence.

'How far was it, Constable, from the top of the first hill to the dip where the cow was?'

'A hundred yards.'

'How far was it from that dip to the top of the next hill?'

'A hundred yards.'

'And how far was it from the top of one hill to the top of the other?'

'A hundred yards.'

'Just a minute constable,' said the judge, 'I want to get some idea of your powers of estimation. How far would you say it is diagonally across this courtroom, by that I mean from *that* corner to *that* corner?'

'A hundred yards.'

'I see. That will be all. No further questions.'

The constable came down proudly to where my father was standing at the back of the court. 'Silly ould bugger on the bench,' he said, 'thought he was going to catch *me* out.'

A-Hunting We Will Go

Our new parochial hall was quite close to the house where we lived, and on frosty nights when there was a dance in progress and the side door was open, you could hear the music of the band.

One night I was standing in our doorway listening and I heard a tune called 'Sail Along Silvery Moon'. It was played as a duet between alto sax and trumpet and I was entranced. I ran up to the hall and stood in the darkness looking in the side door at the band. The priest saw me. 'What are you doing, skulking around out there? Get off home or I'll tell your parents.' It was the first time I had heard the word 'skulking'. But my mind was made up, and a few days later, I went to Belfast on a lorry and purchased a trumpet. I was told that the correct way to

139

learn the trumpet was to play long steady notes to develop a proper tone, but at first it was so loud that I was banished from the house and had to practise outside.

At this time one of the great pastimes in the country was hunting, following hounds on foot as they chased a hare or fox. You could follow the progress of the hunt by listening to the cheering of the huntsmen as they encouraged their hounds from the hilltops. The chief huntsman had a special hunting horn to which the hounds rallied. Several times when I practised my long notes outside, two large dogs with brown and white patches would lope through the hedge at the foot of the garden and come straight up to me looking up expectantly with their tongues hanging out. It was only later that I discovered the reason for their presence. They were beagles belonging to a great huntsman who lived half a mile away across the fields. They had heard the trumpet and thought it was a hunting horn. Fortunately as my playing improved, it sounded more musical and my animal followers stayed at home. But I still had to listen to my tormentor-in-chief after Mass on Sunday.

'I hear you have the gift.'

'What?'

'Some people have it and some haven't.'

'What's that?'

'A way with animals. I hear you had half the hounds in the country round the house with that new trumpet of yours. They might be at the next dance too. What's the priest going to say if half the dancers are dogs? All the best now Bryan, or maybe I should say, tally-ho and hark away!'

Belonging

It was a day when I got caned at school and scolded at home but I remember it as one of the happiest days of my life, a day when I was no longer an outsider, a day when I finally belonged.

All the big boys went to school in bare feet, but I was sent out in boots. I was bitterly ashamed of them, and would hide them under a hedge on the way to school and put them on as I came back home, in order to be like the other boys. I lived near the school and used to go home for my lunch, but I longed to be part of all the happenings at lunchtime.

On dry days the big boys would play hounds and hares over the fields, but on wet days, they would some-times go into the chapel next-door, to 'run the seats'.

They could run in their bare feet from the back to the front of the chapel, across the tops of the backs of the seats, never once touching the floor. Then they would jump off the front seat, and with a nod towards piety, genuflect in front of the tabernacle, run down the aisle and start again. I envied them their skill, and once, in the evening, I sneaked into the chapel, took off my boots and tried it myself, but I fell ignominiously between the seats, and nearly broke my legs. I felt it was a punishment from the Lord, and never had the nerve to attempt it again.

One day when I got back from lunch, there was an ominous silence in the classroom. The boys were sitting apprehensively in the long desks, and at the top of the room was the parish priest, talking in a low venomous whisper to the master. He had thin lips and wore rimless glasses. His eyes were expressionless, like those of a cobra. People said he could look through you. The conversation ended. He jabbed his finger at the master, and said, 'Now do your duty. As for you,' he said looking at us with those snake eyes, 'your parents will hear about this on Sunday, desecrating the Lord's house with your loutish behaviour.' And he stormed out in a whoosh of black robes.

I could hear whispers from the desks ... *'I saw his shadow coming in and I knelt down ... He said it was a sacrilege ... He said it was blasphemy.'* The master said nothing, but went to the press and took out the cane. The boys rubbed their hands together under the desks, knowing what was to come.

'All boys who were in the chapel, line out along the wall,' he said. And with a few practice swings of the cane he started. Every boy got a slap on each hand and a cut across the legs. He was a skilled practitioner and could also catch you on the way back up, a case of buy one get one free.

I watched from the desks until he came to one boy who pulled back his hand every time the master tried to slap him. The came whistled up and down through the empty air. Whenever he tried to cut him across the legs, the lad jumped over the cane, until the air seemed to me to be full of swishing canes and waving arms and dancing feet so that the whole performance became like a demented Nineteen-Fifties version of *Riverdance* . . . and I laughed.

It was there, as they say, that Aughrim was lost. It was out on the floor, join the line and I got my double slap on the hands and a stinging cut across the legs.

On the way home from school, we compared the stripes across our hands and the red weal we all had on our legs. It was the red badge of courage. We were a band of brothers, and I was right there in the middle of them. I said farewell to my comrades-in-arms, and walked barefooted into the house. I had left my boots under the hedge, and my mother drew a deep breath as she started scolding. But I didn't care. At last I belonged.

How Much is that
Doggie in the Window?

In the Fifties, when I was eleven years of age, two men came to our house to ask if I could join a small dance band that had formed in the local area. I was tremendously excited, wondering if I would be allowed, but of course it was a foregone conclusion: in typical country fashion, they had been speaking to my father previously and these were only the formalities.

The older man went into the kitchen to talk to my parents and the younger came into the sitting-room and talked to me of the different dances: quicksteps, slow foxtrots, slow waltzes, tangos, rumbas and sambas. I can still see him beating out the rhythm of the tango with the flat of his hands on his knees as he sat by me at the piano.

I was to make my debut with the Starlight Dance Band in the Star Ballroom, Ballyconnell, on St Patrick's Night. My mother taught me songs such as 'Ramona', 'Can I Forget You', 'Lilli Marlene' and all the Jolson hits. I told all the boys in school.

There was one man in the area who fancied himself as a bit of a wag. After Mass on St Patrick's Day, he came over to me. 'I hear they're taking the roof off the Star Ballroom in Ballyconnell,' he said. This was a disaster, no roof, no dance, no debut.

'Why?' I asked.

'To let in the Starlight,' he said. 'Begod, there'll soon not be a roof left on a hall in the country.' I could cheerfully have strangled him.

And so began my association with the Starlight Dance Band which lasted for twelve years. I soon discovered a number of things about the band. None of them could read music. The sheet music on the stands was just there for show. They used to look at it and pretend they were reading it. The manager stood in the wings and said things like, 'Turn the music an odd time, lads.'

The double bass player had no idea how to play the instrument, but used to stand at the back and pluck the strings in time to the music. Strings were expensive, so when one of them broke, he didn't buy a new one, but knotted the two broken pieces together. One night I looked over and discovered that he was using a length of rope called Hairy Ned, the kind used for tying ricks of hay, as a string.

The other members treated me with paternal tolerance, all except one.

Big Frank delighted in making my life a misery. Sitting beside me in the van, he would punch me repeatedly on the upper arm. Eventually, stung into puny retaliation, I would punch him back, only to find that he had concealed a heavy steel microphone up his sleeve and I would end up with skinned knuckles. I fell for it every time.

Another night when they were telling ghost stories he told one about his grandfather. 'He was coming out of Swanlinbar on a horse one night,' he said, 'when a headless horseman rode up beside him. He kept my grandfather company,' said Frank, 'for a half a mile of the road and then when they came to a gap in the hedge, he turned round, smiled at him, and disappeared into the field.'

I was impressed, until he turned to me and said, 'How could he smile at him if he was headless, you eejit.' And for nights afterwards, he mocked my stupidity.

It wasn't that he was cruel, he just loved 'taking a hand' at people. Our manager always had a fine sense of his own importance. He would be talking to the parish priest in some hall before a dance when Frank would interrupt him:

'Hi Sonny,' he would say, calling him by his country

name which the manager loathed. 'Hi Sonny, where's the switch for this electric?' knowing full well that the hall was lit by gas and that we were going to run the amplification off a twelve-volt battery.

Now Frank had one skill of which he was inordinately proud. None of us could match him, hard though we tried. Four of our members lived near the Bog Cross, and when we arrived there late at night, we would all get out to stretch our legs. The ritual was always the same. The manager, who fancied himself as a bit of a scholar, would always say, 'Well boys, in the words of Shakespeare, "If you have tears, prepare to shed them now".' And we would line up along the hedge and answer Nature's call.

Now Frank's skill was that on occasions such as these he was able to write his name on the road. He could do a beautiful capital F, an artistic loop for the K. But his piece de resistance was that he could put in a full stop – a full stop with no connecting lines to the main word. 'There yez are boys,' he would say. 'Perfect. None of yez can do that.' And he was right. Our efforts to emulate him invariably ended up looking like one of the more abstract of modern paintings.

One St Stephen's night, we had again arrived at the Bog Cross. It was crisp and clear with bright moonlight. Big Frank stood behind the manager when he was making his Shakespearean speech, miming the words over his head to make me laugh, and then we proceeded as usual.

There was a hard frost that night and in the morning, there on the road, written in ice was the name F. R. A. N. K., capital F, extravagantly looped K, isolated full stop and all.

Everybody going the road had a good look. Women got off their bicycles to look at it, children tried to slide on it, men in ass carts took the pipes out of their mouths and smiled grimly when they saw it, the schoolmaster, who liked a drink, said in the pub that it was a fine example of the art of calligraphy. But Frank's little son brought home from school a note from the infant teacher that was as frosty as the weather, and Frank brought a bucket of water up from the house and poured it over it to turn it into a solid sheet of ice.

And somehow, my life in the band got a lot easier after that.

To learn the hit tunes of the time called for some ingenuity, since there were few radios and fewer telephones. One of the band, who had a keen ear, would get a message: 'Go up to the shop quickly. There's a telephone call for you.' On the other end of the line would be his cousin who worked in England. She would sing the latest hit to him and he would remember the melody while the shop girl wrote down the words on a teabag. Then at the next practice, we would all learn it from him.

We all played the hit tunes of the time which we

learned from Radio Luxembourg. Looking back, I now realize that the past is definitely another country. I can hardly believe the innocence. We would sing, 'How much is that Doggie in the Window?' and everybody in the hall would shout 'Bow-wow!'

Mind you, I often thought that if you were dancing with a girl, that song was a good barometer as to how you were getting on. If you sang 'How Much is that Doggie in the Window?', and she looked up at you and said 'Bow-wow', you could . . . open negotiations. Or can you credit that we sang nonsense such as 'Mairzy doats and dozy doats and liddle lamzy divet, a kiddlely divey too, wouldn't you?' I remember solemn discussions as to what it meant. 'You see,' someone would say, 'it means mares eat oats and does eat oats and little lambs eat ivy, a kid will eat ivy too, wouldn't you?'

And at school, I could show off, because I knew the words of the latest hits, even nonsense words like 'Gilly Gilly Ossenfeffer Katzenellen Bogen by the Sea.' Or, mightily daring, the words of songs that were banned by the church. 'Give me five minutes more, only five minutes more, Give me five minutes more in your arms,' or 'Put another nickel in, in the nickelodeon, All I want is lovin' you and music, music, music.'

However, what I remember most clearly are the lessons I learned about dealing with the public. One night, in the middle of a tune, towards the end of the dance, the saxophone player's instrument finally gave up the ghost. He was our best player and I thought we were finished. But no – 'Give me the double bass,' he said.

Now I knew he could no more play it than I could, but he took it straight out to the front of the stage. He smiled down at the dancers, and with an appearance of the utmost enjoyment, started plucking the strings in time to the beat; he twirled it around, slapped it on the back, pretended to put it under his chin, put it down sideways and mimed riding it like a horse. A crowd gathered round to watch his antics and he got a huge round of applause when the tune was finished. One man said to me, 'Who's your man on the big bull fiddle? Begod, he can handle her.'

Band practice was held in rotation in the houses of the various members, all of whom lived close together, except me. It meant a cycle ride of three miles each way for me, and when the practice was over, they would tell ghost stories. I realize now that they were solely for my benefit, for I was the only one who had to travel home in the dark. Apparently the countryside was thickly populated with ghosts, banshees and fairies, all on my way home. There was a ghost at the Stone Depot, and one at the Pound Cross, and one at the Preaching House, and the door of Patton's house always had to be left open because it was built over a fairy path and if they closed the door, the house would crack from top to bottom. The father of one of the members, taking a shortcut on the way home late at night, had stepped on a 'stray sod' and found himself trapped in a field surrounded by thick, high whitehorn hedges and it was only when he took off his coat and turned it inside out and put it back on again that he found his way out. And two men on their way home from a wake not a hundred yards from this house had heard the banshee crying in a field called the Fuireann Oir. 'You'll pass it on the way home,' they said helpfully.

A ghostly horse and carriage used to go down the Old Road, and a woman I knew well who lived three fields away used to lie awake on frosty nights and listen to the rumble of the wheels and the jingle of the haness and the sound of the horse's hooves. When I was leaving, I used to open the door and stare apprehensively out into the rectangle of darkness and look back longingly into the Tilley-lit kitchen, before getting my bicycle. 'All the best,' they would say, 'safe home now.'

One dark windy night, after one of these sessions, as I was cycling home with no light on my bicycle, head down against the wind, I heard a loud snort in the air above my head. I was utterly terrified, wobbled violently and fell off the bicycle. When I looked up, I could make out the shadowy figure of a horse, enormous against the scudding clouds, and immediately I had visions of it rearing up, with a ghostly hooded rider waiting to sweep me off, but then I realized with weak-kneed relief that the animal was standing with its tail to the hedge and its head towards the centre of the road. In the dark, I had cycled unseeingly under its neck and it had snorted in fear. That, I thought, made two of us, as I shakily continued my journey home.

And then came electricity. An old man said to me recently, 'The electric light put an end to the ghosts.' Not everybody welcomed it. One woman said that it showed up the dirt in corners of the kitchen that hadn't been cleaned for years and that it gave her a mountain of extra work to do. Another said, 'It's great. Powerful handy when you'd be looking for the lamp oil.'

Other, more subtle changes occurred. It had always been the custom that when a neighbour came in, he was immediately offered a cup of tea. This had become something of a ritual, and there were various conventions to be gone through. First of all it was necessary for the offer to be refused. 'Ah no, I couldn't. I'm just rising from the table.' (For some reason this always made me think of the person in the shape of a balloon.) 'Ah sure I'm only putting you to bother.' But the rules of hospitality dictated that he would be forced. 'Sure it's only a drop in your hand,' and with a show of reluctance he would eventually accept.

Then came the ceremony of building up the hearth fire with extra sods of turf, hanging the kettle above it from the crook and waiting for it to boil. Finally, the tea was wetted, a drop poured out on the hearth, and the tea-drinking would begin.

I remember a rather pompous friend of mine, who regarded himself as an intellectual, remarking to one woman, 'How wonderful. A libation to the gods.'

'What?' she said.

'The pouring of the tea on to the hearth. An ancient pagan custom, offering the first portion to the gods to bring good fortune.'

'Boys oh boys,' said the woman, 'and there was me thinking that I was just seeing if it was strong enough.'

After the arrival of electricity, I was present when one man started laughing when the woman plugged in an electric kettle to boil on the table. I asked him what he was laughing at.

He said, 'What would the ould people say, boiling the kettle on the table?'

What indeed.

For us in the band, the coming of electricity was a boon. No longer did we have to haul in heavy car batteries to power the microphones. And we also could purchase, oh the luxury of it, a *tape-recorder*, with which to record the Top Twenty hits from Radio Luxembourg.

Not everybody fully understood the workings of this piece of technology. On one occasion we recorded an old fiddler playing a reel, and then played it back to him.

He listened in astonishment. 'Well that's a terror,' he said. 'It's amazing. Do you know it played it damn nearly as well as I played it myself!'

By now, we were travelling distances of up to fifty miles to play at dances. Sometimes we would leave while it was still daylight and men would be working in the fields, planting potatoes or mowing with scythes. One man told me recently that he used to watch us going off in the van and thought that we must have been the happiest people in the whole world and that he would have given anything to have been going with us, because to him we represented freedom and the outside world.

'I watched the van disappearing round a turn in the road,' he said, 'and I looked at the wet rushes I had to mow and I thought I would die with misery.' Sometimes the mowers would stop to look at us, some of them sharpening the blade with a scythestone. I learned that it was the sure sign of a lazy man if he spent too much time sharpening the blade.

One night, in a dancehall far away in the County Leitrim, there was nobody in the hall and we were practising before the dance began. We played the same eight bars over and over, but just could not get it right. Eventually one of the doormen came up to the stage and said, 'Right lads, that's enough of the sharpenin', what about a bit of the mowin'?'

*　　*　　*

When I went to university, I used to come home on a scooter to play at weekends. On long journeys in the van, I sat and listened for hours as the band talked. It was for me a different kind of university. We were all young, the future lay sparkling before us and I thought we would be together for ever.

Coping the Lea

He was already in the field with the ass and cartload of manure when I arrived on the bicycle, panting from the climb up the mountain road. He handed me a graip. The shaft had been roughly cut out of the hedge and one of the four prongs was broken. The manure steamed and smelt to high heaven.

'Man, that's sweet dung,' he said.

We were going to set potatoes in new uncultivated ground, making ridges with spades, 'coping the lea', as he described it. Far away below us, Lough Erne and its islands glistened like a necklace in the morning sunlight.

'That's a great view,' I said.

'You can't live on scenery,' he replied.

He produced a ball of the rope we called 'Hairy Ned'.

There were two short pointed sticks attached to it and he directed me to walk down the field, unrolling the rope as I went. He stuck one of the sticks in the ground and shouted to me to do the same, directing me to the precise spot.

He went to the hedge and with his tobacco knife he cut a straight stick of hazel, measured it on his arm and cut it off at the right length. 'Three foot two inches,' he said, the width of the ridge and furrow. All morning we spread the manure with mathematical precision until the field was covered in brown stripes, each one identical to the others. Lunch was cold tea and white-loaf bread and homemade butter with streaks of grey through it. We ate silently and I noticed his gnarled fingers, his broken nails, and his hands, clawed from a lifetime of gripping the shaft of a spade. And I recalled what I had heard about him. In his youth, he had been known as a tremendous worker but he had no idea of social etiquette. When he went to his first dance, he wore the same clothes he had worn during the week and the only preparation he made was to kick his boots against the side of the hall to knock off the rough stuff. No girl would dance with him, and when he had been refused for the third time, he stood back and said, 'Let me tell you miss I could graip dung with any man in this hall,' and had walked out never to return. He had lived alone for forty years.

After lunch he went to the cart and produced a bag

of purple potatoes all of which had been cut in half and dusted with lime. Cuts, he called them.

'You can't beat the blue spud,' he said, and showed me how to put the cuts on the manure, in a series of diamond shapes. Several times he moved my cuts so that the distance between them was inch-perfect. It was like a ritual. His clawed hands handled the potatoes as tenderly as a mother with her baby.

Finally came the actual making of the ridges. 'You're lefthanded,' he said as he handed me a spade. 'You go on that side.'

I watched as he sliced through a rush bush as neatly as a surgeon with a scalpel. A few movements with the spade levered against his inside leg and the sod came up over the manure as if it was on a hinge. He repeated the process and the second sod fitted perfectly on to the first. It looked so easy. I nicked as I had seen him do but when I tried to lift the sod it would not budge. I heaved and hoked and lifted and eventually got the sod up in bits and pieces. He looked at my efforts and said mildly, 'Try and not break the sod.'

He was halfway up the ridge, his side neat and straight, and he came down to me. He looked at the ragged mess I had made and with his heel he kicked the edge into some degree of straightness.

'What matter,' I said petulantly, 'if the ridges aren't straight. Sure the spuds will grow straight anyway.'

He looked at me in amazement. 'Sure you'd be scandalled over the country,' he said.

By mid-afternoon, my back was aching, my schoolboy's soft hands were blistered and caked with dried manure but I was beginning to get the hang of it.

'You're mending,' he said. 'Let the spade do the work.'

When the sun was setting behind the rim of the mountain, we had finished. We threw the graips and spades and rope into the asscart and headed out the gap. We looked back, he with an expression almost of love on his face. The setting sun picked up the shadows of the ridges, brown, straight as corduroy, a work of art, I thought.

That was half a century ago. He is long dead, the man who didn't know he was an artist. The mountain face is covered with a coniferous slum of forestry. There are neat paths through it and picnic tables. But you can't see Lough Erne, and tall trees cover the field where once I watched a small sensitive man coping the lea, with the skill and the pride of centuries.

The Wet Winding Roads

There were certain houses in the country that were noted as 'ceili houses', houses where people would visit and where there would always be a welcome, and conversation and entertainment. I have always looked back on travelling with the band as being in a sort of ceili house on wheels. We talked of everything, of football and feats of strength, of tragedies and murders, ghosts and farming and fairy forts and emigration, and always, always, the quality of the land that we were passing through.

I remember once, we stopped to ask the way of a man who was digging potatoes. Not because we were lost, but out of sheer curiosity to see what kind of potatoes he had.

'What are the spuds like?' asked our manager, John Joe.

'Poor enough,' said the man. 'One here and one there. What are they like in your country?'

'Worse,' said John Joe. 'One here and none there.'

Across half a century I can recall scraps and fragments of conversation I heard, like the legendary Big Tom Maguire, who was the strongest man in three parishes, and who at the age of sixteen had choked a huge fox to death that he found killing the hens in his mother's henhouse. He played for the legendary Harps football team and had a reputation for having a fearsome shot. One day the opposing goalie took one look at him coming with the ball and ran sideways out of the goal to escape, because he had heard that Tom had once broken a man's ribs with the ball, and as he said himself, he didn't want to be killed.

And we heard about a big family who were all great singers, and when the first of them was going to America, they had a party for him the night before, an American wake. When he had to leave early in the morning in a pony and trap to the station, the whole family went outside and clasped hands in a circle and in the grey dawn light they sang together for the last time, their favourite song, 'The Hills of Glenswilly':

The Wet Winding Roads

No more, no more 'neath the sycamore
I'll hear the blackbird sing
No more to me the brown cuckoo will welcome
  back the Spring
No more I'll plough your fertile fields, a 'chuisle
  geal mo chree'
On a foreign soil I'm doomed to toil
Far, far from Glenswilly

It was the saddest thing ever seen.

They're all gone now . . . the house is down . . . I could show you where it was . . .

It's a long journey home. Gradually the talk dies away. Sleeping forms slouch uncomfortably over instruments. The night miles slip away. And so does our youth.

Oh the wet winding roads
Brown bogs with black water
And my thoughts on white ships
And the King of Spain's daughter

Hob-nailed Boots

FOR SALE – BOOTS
7 rows of good Irish Hobs
Toe Plates, Heel Tips, Toe Caps 31/6
Boots. Light for Sunday wear
Sparabled for fair and market
Nailed for the land

In the Fifties you would still see advertisements such as this, for hob-nailed boots. But they were reaching the end of their shelf-life, and for good wear we bright young fellows wore what we called 'low shoes'. It was thus shod, that in the year of our Lord, one thousand nine hundred and fifty-four, I attended my very first dance in the Rainbow Ballroom, Glenfarne, County Leitrim, The

Ballroom of Romance. Nine of us there were in a black Volkswagen Beetle and the last ones had to get in head first. It was clear and frosty when we parked a hundred yards from the hall and as we climbed stiffly out we could hear the MC announcing the dances.

A group of young lads arrived on bicycles and flung them into the hedge. We all started to run towards the hall, the cyclists with the hoppity genuflecting gait that results when you are trying to run and take off your bicycle clips at the same time! At the door we were met by a blast of hot air, and a smell of perfume and powder and perspiration and we were were so excited that we could hardly get the money out of our pockets. And when we finally got into the hall what did we do? We stood in lines and looked across at the girls and they stood in lines and looked back at us.

Suddenly as if by signal there was a charge by the men, that, as one man said, nearly took the sidewall out of the hall. It took me completely by surprise. I was swept across the floor and ended up behind the the line of girls looking back out. My next attempt to ask a girl to dance ended when a male arm reached across me and grabbed the girl of my choice by the shoulder and pulled her on to the dance floor. But eventually I got the hang of it.

There were three big raw-boned fellows in the hall. Somebody said that they came from a mountainy far-back part of the country. They stood in a group close together, their collars open at the neck. They smoked cigarettes in cupped hands, talked to each other out of the side of their mouths and to our amusement they wore hob-nailed boots. About the middle of the night's dancing, one of them came over to me.

'How're you goin' on?' he said.

'OK,' I said.

'Do you see that girl that you were dancin' with?'

'Yes,' I said.

'Well, the brother, that's the big red-haired fellow over there smokin' the cigarette, was dancin' with her earlier.'

'But . . .' I began.

'He'll be dancin' with her again, do you understand?'

And he walked away. When he had gone a few steps, he stopped, turned round, looked me in the eyes, nodded meaningfully and said, 'Ye boy ye.'

Don Corleone couldn't have done it better. I was never as terrified in my life. I would love to say that I went ahead and danced with the girl anyway, but I learned one thing that Christmas night. When it comes to emotions, fear is stronger than romance. And a Don Corleone in hob-nailed boots quickly puts ideas of romance out of your head!

Bonny Mary of Argyll

There was a custom in our part of the country that if you were asked to sing at a country house dance, you first refused and after much forcing you consented, a bit like the formalities involved in being offered a cup of tea. Normally the singer remained seated, took off his cap, leaned forward, put his elbow on his knee, and fixed his eyes on a spot on the floor about three feet in front of him. He sang the entire song to this spot, occasionally nodding his head diagonally to emphasise the more important words. The audience sat in respectful silence, and in between verses they would shout encouragement, usually by saying his full name:

'Good man John Maguire.'

'That man can sing.'

'A terror, a holy terror.'

I often thought it sounded like prayer meetings of black Americans.

It was also the custom to insert a nasal 'N' sound into words with a long vowel, so that even in the chapel choir, you would hear, 'Holy Gond we praise thy name.'

When the singer came to the last line, it was for some reason always spoken, not sung, followed by self-criticism of the quality of his singing something like this: 'And when Dalton dined the banshee crined' (sung) 'in the valley of Knockanure ah sure I can sing none' (spoken). The whole audience would immediately contradict him and reassure him about the quality of his music.

'Well begod you can.'

'That was as well sung as ever I heard it.'

'Sure it's in the breed of you to be a singer, your mother was the girl could sing.'

'Aye and he had an uncle on the father's side, a real tipper on the accordion.'

I was present when one man got a ferocious punch in the face at one particular dance. He didn't like the singer and when the man said, 'I can sing none,' this man muttered, 'Well that's the truth anyway,' not realising that the singer's brother was sitting beside him.

One night on the way home from playing, there was a bit of silence in the van, and suddenly, the manager said with mock formality, 'I now call upon the driver, Mr James Gunn, for his pleasure.'

I was waiting for the ritual show of reluctance and the chorus of persuasion. But no, this was different. There were a few seconds of silence and then Jimmy launched straight into 'Bonny Mary of Argyll':

I have heard the Mavis singing her love song to the morn,
I have seen the dewdrop clinging to the rose just newly born.

It was a lovely song and Jimmy had a rich rolling voice with a hint of vibrato. He sang, as my mother would have said, 'with great feeling' and he had a fine sense of performance. When he came to the end, there was none of the business of speaking the last line. On the last 'Mary of Argyll', up an octave he went and finished with both syllables of the world 'Argyll' lengthened and broadened like an operatic singer finishing an aria. Crescendo, rallentando, allargando, he had the lot.

Needless to say, he got the Starlight equivalent of a standing ovation. For some reason, I always remember that night, the hum of the engine as the miles slipped away beneath the wheels, the huddled listening faces reflected in the greenish light from the dashboard. And I never hear that song but I think of Jimmy Gunn.

'Twas your voice my gentle Mary, and your artless
winning smile,
That have made this world an Eden, Bonny Mary
of Argyll.

The Boat

Arthur was a small cantankerous little man who lived near the lough shore. Even though he was as poor as a church mouse, he was bursting with pride in himself and his breed. In particular, he was proud of his nephew Sean, the golden boy, tall and handsome, who lived nearby, and owned the best donkey in the country. He would boast about him in all the houses in the neighbourhood. All except that of his next-door neighbour Peter, for Arthur and Peter were deadly enemies in the way only next-door neighbours can be. Peter was quiet and shrewd.

But the real trouble began when Arthur bought a boat. Not a new one, a fourteen-foot wooden boat which he turned upside down and painted lovingly and moored at the bottom of the meadow down in front of his house.

He didn't use it very much but he loved the idea of it, and especially the fact that it would annoy Peter.

They both had plots of potato ground, some distance away from their houses, separated by a wide mearin drain, and in the springtime they would go down the lane to these plots and work on opposite sides of the drain, never speaking one word to each other. When a neighbour called to see how the work was going, Arthur brought up the topic of the boat in conversation.

'Caught a big pike yesterday when I was out in the boat,' he said loudly so that Peter would hear. 'No use living near the lough if you haven't a boat.'

Young Sean, his nephew, working in his own plot, listened and said nothing. But mischief was afoot.

That night, a group of young conspirators gathered in Sean's house and planned a shocking deed. Some time later, half a dozen ghostly figures could be seen leaving the house and going out into the April moonlight. They were carrying with them the collar and hames of the donkey and they headed straight for the field where the animal stood like a silver statue. They harnessed it, led it to the shore and attached the reins to a hook on the front of Arthur's boat, dragged it out of the water, and across the bottom of the meadow in the direction of the plots. When they came to the lane, they were afraid that the donkey's hooves would be heard so they lifted the boat bodily over their heads and walked down the lane with only their legs visible, like some giant insect. One of them, a timid soul, carried the oars and the rowlocks behind the solemn procession till they came to the vegetable plots.

They dropped the boat into the drain between the plots of the deadly enemies. It fitted snugly and they arranged the oars artistically so that it looked as if someone was about to take a stroke. Then they silently dispersed across the moonlit fields.

Next morning they were waiting, hidden in the bushes to see what would happen. Arthur came down the lane, head bent forward, carrying on his back a bag of seed potatoes for planting. He didn't see the boat until the last minute. His eyes and mouth opened wide, the bag fell off his back, potatoes rolling in all directions. He lifted his hat with his two hands, scratched his head violently and immediately set off running. They could hear him ranting and raving at Peter's door even though they were hundreds of yards away.

That night there was a knock on young Sean's door. It was Peter. 'You heard about Arthur's boat, Sean,' he said.

'I did,' said Sean.

'It's a curious thing,' said Peter, looking at Sean with gimlet eyes, 'but I was down at the lough shore where that boat was and I seen the tracks of a newly shod ass leading across the bottom of that meadow in the direction of them plots. You know, Sean, nobody else round here bothers shoeing their ass, except yourself.'

And he left. The boat stayed in that drain all summer, and Arthur worked alongside and never once looked near it, and never once was he heard to mention it ever again. When the winter floods filled the drain, it floated once more, rocking gently on the water, and the following spring it settled down again in the mud on the bottom. The next winter it didn't rise because it was beginning to rot and it filled with water and soon only the ribs were left, and the grass and weeds grew over it and it disappeared for ever.

The Stonemason

I suppose there's one in every village; someone whom people regard as a fool, or possibly a knave, and so it was with old Mick the stonemason.

He lived alone in a small two-roomed house that he had built himself, and it was said that he wore the same clothes, day and night. His hair was long and dirty, grey and sparse, and he combed it across the top of his head to disguise the bald patches, the whole coiffure being kept in place with a net more commonly used for holding onions in the local shop, topped by a filthy hat. One man said that he only took the hat off in two places, in bed and at Mass. And, he added, he sleeps in both places.

You always got the impression that Mick was secretly laughing at something, that he found the world a slightly ludicrous place to live in, and I always felt that he was the living embodiment of the old saw, 'It takes a wise man to play the fool'. Once I heard him demolish a smart-alec who was poking fun at him at a country-house dance by standing up with great dignity and saying, 'It's not the man that has the most that gives the most away It's not the man that knows the most that has the most to say.'

He was supposed to be a master mason, and always claimed to have sculpted a stone head that stood outside the local barracks. Even when the curator of the Ulster museum came down from Belfast and dated it from the seventeenth century, he was completely unfazed, and inverted the argument nicely by asking, 'What would she know, be the jay she wasn't around three hundred years ago.'

And the strange thing was that people believed him. 'That man is a genius,' they would say. 'Only for the drink, he could have built St Paul's Cathedral.'

And indeed he was fond of the drink. He would work for a few days and then would go missing, on his holidays, as he described his binges, sleeping away from home, in a turfhouse, a hayshed or barn.

'I only drink,' he said once, 'on two occasion; when I'm thirsty, and when I'm not.'

Now our local shopkeeper was also the undertaker and upholstered his own coffins. I remember as a child, going up the wooden steps that led to the dimly-lit loft where he stored the coffins in rows on trestles, and watching him at work, stapling in the satin lining and putting a sort of pillow in one end. 'To make it comfortable for him,' he said to me grimly. He told me that on one memorable occasion, he brought a customer to select a coffin for his deceased mother. As they entered the loft, the man's eyes hadn't got used to the semi-darkness, and peering at the ghostly rows on the trestles, he saw the lid of one of the coffins slowly lifting and a figure sat up. The poor man fainted, but it was only Mick, sleeping off the effects of a heavy bout of drinking in a soft well-upholstered bed.

'I have the place warm for him anyway,' he said to the undertaker as he walked past.

One day Mick was working for the priest and the Angelus bell rang. Both men crossed themselves, but long after the priest had finished, Mick was only halfway through and even after he had blessed himself, he had several other mutterings to do before he finally replaced his hat.

'You're very fond of your prayers, Mick,' said the priest.

'Father,' he replied, 'I love the Angelus but be the jay I hate the Rosary.'

When evening time came, the priest produced no money, but said, 'Thank you, Mick, and may you have God's blessing.'

Mick said, 'Ah sure, Father, my pockets are full of it.'

On another occasion he was in a house where people were talking about lonesome things. One man said that the saddest thing he ever saw was at the funeral of a young girl who had been killed in an accident. Another said that the saddest thing that he ever saw was leaving people to the train on their way to America. They asked Mick for his contribution.

'Well I'll tell yez,' he said. 'There was one day I was clampin' turf in the bog and in the heel of the evenin', when the shadows were getting long, I sat down with my back against a clamp of turf and put my jacket round my shoulders. I got out the plug tobacco and cut off a bit with my knife. I teased it up nicely in my hand and then I filled up the pipe and tapped it down in the bowl and then I got a stiff cushog of grass and pushed it up the stem to make sure it was clear and then I put my hand in my trousers pocket, and then I searched my jacket pocket, and then I searched my waistcoat pocket.' He paused. 'And I had no matches,' he said. 'And do you know,' said he, 'be the jay, that was the lonesomest thing I ever saw.'

Then came the day when he fell off a ladder, sprained his ankle, and had to go to the doctor. He was strongly advised to wash his feet, but ever the economist, he washed only the injured one. The doctor examined him and then said, 'Could I have a look at the other foot to see how badly swollen this one is by comparison?'

Mick took off his boot and sock and showed him. The doctor looked.

'My God,' he said, 'they're not comrades at all. Are you piebald?'

In some ways a creature of habit, he used to visit a certain house every week. He would sit by the fire, saying nothing and letting the conversation swirl around him. But one night some of the young people there poked just a bit too much fun at him and he left, vowing never to go back. Diplomatic messages were sent to him and emissaries dispatched and eventually he relented and returned. Everyone made a great fuss of him. The dog whined a welcome and wagged his tail and licked his hand. (They say every dog likes a fool.)

The woman of the house said, 'There you are now, Mick, we're all glad to see you, even the dog is glad to see you.'

'The dog,' said Mick, 'is the only one that means it.'

Disgrace

It was a great house for dances. People said that there was a horse's skull under the hearthstone for the sole purpose of amplifying the sound made by hob-nailed boots when men were dancing. The best dancers could rise sparks off the concrete floor and could do a rat-tat-tat with their metal-shod heels like a kettle drum. Sadly, I have to confess that it was in that house that one night, at the age of fourteen, I disgraced myself, not once, not twice, but three different times.

The format of the country-house dances was always the same, a quarter-barrel of porter in the corner, lashings of food handed round, poteen surreptitiously supplied, music from fiddles and accordions, dancing and singing. Every singer had his own song so you knew in advance what they were going to sing. One man sang 'The County of Tyrone'. There was a line which went, 'They took me away to Derry gaol from the county of Tyrone.' But he sang, 'They took me away to Derry gaol in the county of Tyrone,' and I sniggered. Everybody looked at me and I blushed.

Next up was an elderly man who, filled with importance and with drink, announced, 'Well boys, I'll sing yez a tragedy. It's about the war in the Crimeay.'

The young lad sitting next to me nudged me in the ribs; I was fit to explode but had managed to contain myself until the singer came to a line which ran, 'The rifles flashed and the cannon crashed and the balls they fell like rain.' It was too much for me and I burst out into uncontrollable laughter. The singer stopped in a huff and it was only after abject apologies on my part and several glasses of whiskey that he deigned to continue while I could hear remarks about myself which mainly conveyed that 'yon buck has no manners.'

But worse was to follow. Everyone called Mick the stonemason Tarry-Toory-Too because he was always humming the same song, 'The Valley of Knockanure'. 'Tarry Toory Toory Tootoory Toory Totoory To Toory To.'

'Do you like that song, Mick?' someone would ask.

'A pure beauty,' he would say, 'sure it's a pure beauty.'

Now present on this night was a young man from

across the border in Cavan who had come into the country as a labouring boy, and someone said that he could sing. After the usual ritual persuasion, he took off his cap, turned sideways to the audience, put his elbow on his knee, stared meaningfully at a spot on the floor about three feet in front of him, and started. The song he sang was 'The Valley of Knockanure'. As was the custom, he spoke the last line and criticized his own singing ability; 'And the banshee cried when young Dalton died. (Speaking) "In the Valley of Knockanure", ah sure I can sing none, sure I forgot the half of it.'

Everyone leaped in to assure him that he was great and the breed of him was musical and have a glass of porter and come up to the room and have something warmer. All this while, old Mick was sitting there turning his hat round and round on his knee. Then he stood up, and said with immense dignity, 'A man would have a song no time till the country would have it,' put his hat on his head and walked out.

And I laughed.

I didn't realize that a major diplomatic incident had taken place until the woman of the house said to her husband, 'Go on quick, bring him back.'

A couple of respectable men went out the door and the woman turned to me and said witheringly, 'There's nothing funny about it. Some people shouldn't be let near dances.' A few minutes tension followed until we again heard voices and in they all came with Mick in the middle of them. The young labouring man went to him and apologized profusely saying, 'I didn't know it was your song.'

But Mick was gracious. 'You sang the song very well,' he said, 'damn nearly as well as I would sing it myself.'

Some Enchanted Evening

There is a road near where I was reared which is half a mile in length and straight as an arrow. It was constructed as relief work in famine times but it is still called the New Line. Bridges across the lough that were built in 1933 are still called the New Bridges, and the parochial hall, built in 1947, is to this day called the New Hall. When it was first opened it attracted huge crowds, but as the years went by, they became smaller and smaller. People said that the New Hall was like the *Titanic*, it was going down.

Then in the Fifties a new curate arrived, and he saw it as his mission in life to bring the crowds back. His strategy was simple. At each dance he would have a special attraction, a guest artiste. These were never from the top flight of performers but they had associations with them. There was Bridie Gallagher's niece, Ruby Murray's cousin, Eileen Donaghy's sister. Usually we tolerated these as a necessary interruption to the serious business of getting girls.

Then one Sunday he announced that for the big Christmas dance, there would be a well-known Dublin singer, Mr John Mansfield, coming that night to the hall and that he hoped there would be a huge crowd. Nobody had ever heard of the man.

The band that night, I remember, was The Des Treacy Trio, accordion, drums and singer, who played old-time waltzes and quicksteps and Irish music. Halfway through the dance the curate came out on to the stage.

'Now will you put your hands together,' he said, 'and give a nice warm welcome to our guest artiste, Mr John Mansfield,' and to our astonishment, on to the stage walked a large portly man dressed in morning suit with tails, white bow tie and carrying music in his hand.

'Where's the accompanist?' he boomed, every word picked up by the microphone.

The priest was clearly taken aback. 'Well, maybe we could get Des to play the accordion with you,' he stammered.

'I will not be accompanied by an accordion,' said the man. 'Have you a piano?'

'Well, yes,' said the priest hesitantly.

'I'll accompany myself,' declared the great man grandly.

The priest leaned down off the stage and said to me, 'You and Sean bring out the piano from behind the scenery,' and we did.

The front was missing, wires stuck out waving like tentacles as we wheeled it on stage, the keys were yellow and many of them were stuck in the 'down' position. When we placed the piano stool in front of it, a cloud of dust rose from the ancient velvet covering. The audience observed all this silently, and gravely they watched the great man sit down and flick his tails so that they hung down over the back of the piano stool. He shot his cuffs, raised both hands high above the keyboard and brought them down with a dramatic opening chord. Well, it would have been dramatic except that the piano sounded like one of the honky-tonk ones you would hear playing in the Western saloon just before the bad guy walked through the batwing doors.

Then he turned to the audience and in a rich fruity baritone voice, sang, '*Some enchanted evening* –' more dramatic chords. '– *You may see a stranger . . .*'

This went on for four or five lines, and then someone at the back cheered, a short, staccato, 'Yo!' It was immediately answered from the side of the hall with a double-syllabled 'Yo-Ho!' In one second the whole place was in uproar. Amidst the cheering and yelling you could hear shouts of, 'You'll see no strangers here,' 'Get back to

Dublin ye boy ye, you and your swallow tails,' and 'Play us "The Sally Gardens".'

The singer got up and walked off the stage. The priest came out and said, 'Now put your hands together for Mr John Mansfield,' and then down to me said in desperation, 'Would you go and get Des back on as quick as you can.'

For days afterwards, the New Hall was the sole topic of conversation, and strangely enough, the crowds started coming back.

Lost in Collooney

Christmas was the busy time for the thousands of dance bands which crisscrossed the roads of Ireland in the Fifties. All the emigrants would be home and the dance-hall was the place where they would come to enjoy themselves. One year our own small dance band played for twenty-one nights in a row over the festive season and I was staggering by the time we had finished.

For us who lived north of the border it was a frequent occurrence to be stopped and searched by the police, army or the B-Specials, who had a reputation for sectarianism. One night we crossed the border to play in a small parish hall in the west of County Sligo. We had never been there before but some expert told us of a shortcut by which we could avoid going into Sligo town.

It was a night of dense fog and we got hopelessly lost in the maze of small roads with the result that we arrived an hour and a half late. The hall was three quarters full and we faced a sea of hostile faces, big strong young lads home from England, with a few drinks in them, ready, as one of our number said, to gut us. The parish priest was pacing up and down the hall and he tore over to us, purple in the face, apoplectic with rage.

'What kept you?' he demanded. 'What the hell kept you?'

There was a hostile muttering from the crowd and I thought we would never get out of there without being lynched. Now our manager was an older and wiser man than the rest of us and he took the parish priest by the arm over to one side of the hall.

'Do you know, Father,' he said, 'we're lucky to be here at all. We were taken into the barracks by the B-men and we had an awful job getting out.'

It was exactly the right thing to say. The priest went up to the stage and announced this over the microphone. We were instant heroes. The audience burst into cheers and the priest got quite carried away and described us as 'the boys who had broken out of the North'. We could do no wrong and some of them sat on the edge of the stage and listened to us as we played.

We used to play the Jim Reeves number, 'He'll Have To Go', and when our lead singer who had a wonderful bass voice sang the last low note of the line 'I'll tell the man to turn the juke box way down *low*,' one man called me down and said, 'Do you know, it would take two ordinary men to get down to that note.'

I am ashamed to say that we milked the situation unmercifully. It was one of the best nights we ever had and at the end when we played the National Anthem every one stood ramrod straight to attention until the last note had died away. They carried out our instruments and helped us to pack the van and said, 'Ye're great lads and ye're having it tough.'

The fog was denser than ever and the priest told us, 'When you get to Collooney, turn right, and then right again and that will bring you out on your road for the north. Happy Christmas,' he said, '*Slan abhaile.*'

Off we started, everyone peering through the front window barely able to see the sides of the road through the whiteness in front of us. We got to Collooney and turned right and then right again and then we saw a donkey lying on the grass at the side of the road. After driving for another bit, we saw another ass also lying on the grass and we remarked on the coincidence. It was only when we saw the third ass that we realized what was happening. We were driving round in circles. The driver was so angry that he stopped the van, jumped out, kicked the animal to its feet and said, 'There you bugger, you won't be lying there when we come round the next time!'

Noreen Bawn

There seemed to be a lost generation when we played at the dances in North Leitrim in the early Fifties. Everybody was either old or very young. The old couples would sit side by side on the long benches around the hall, occasionally getting up to dance an old-time waltz, moving stiffly like marionettes. The youngsters would jump about in a corner practising their steps and giggling. There were no twenty- or thirty-year-olds. As soon as they reached adulthood, it seemed, they were away, to England mostly, and you wouldn't see them again until they came home for Christmas.

Many of the popular songs of the day were about emigration, some were funny like 'Mursheen Durkin' but most were sad and a big hit of the time was 'Noreen

Bawn'. It told the story of a young girl who emigrated leaving behind her widowed mother. Years passed and one day a beautifully dressed maiden came to the woman's door. It was her daughter but she was dying of consumption. The song ended with the broken-hearted mother praying at her daughter's grave and saying, ''Twas the curse of emigration left you here my Noreen Bawn.'

It sounds sentimental and sloppy to us in this the age of the Celtic Tiger but in the Fifties it was all too real, and when we sang the song, the old couples would stare fixedly at the stage and think their own private thoughts.

One night we were playing in Aughnasheelin and there was a young girl there. I guessed she was about eighteen. She had a head of rich thick auburn hair, done in a slightly old-fashioned style, like you would see in youthful photographs of your mother. She smiled up at me as she danced with her father. At supper for the band after the dance she was there helping. When she poured my tea, she stood behind me and put her hand on my shoulder.

'Will you be here the next night we are back?' I asked.

'No,' she said, 'I am going to Birmingham in the morning.'

As we left, she turned round from the sink where she was washing the dishes and waved a suds-covered hand to me.

'Good luck in Birmingham,' I said.

At Christmas, we were back in Aughnasheelin. The hall was full because all the English ones were there, easily distinguishable by their modern clothes. At first I didn't recognize her. Her hair had been cut short and it was bleached. Her face was heavily and inexpertly made up, and she was smoking. She talked and danced animatedly with her partners. She looked up at the stage but gave no sign of recognizing me. At half-time I went down to the mineral bar and she was there surrounded by predatory males. Her eyes were bright and in the midst of all the soft Leitrim tones, I could hear that her accent was the whine of the British Midlands. I picked up the word Birmingham.

'What's wrong with you,' said the rest of the band members when I got back to the stage. 'You're in the worst of bad form.'

When we played Noreen Bawn that night, she was dancing in the arms of one of the predatory males.

I never saw her again. I cannot even picture her face, but over the half-century that has passed, I sometimes think about her and the tresses of rich dark hair that she left on the floor of an English hairdressing salon and recall her parents' troubled eyes that Christmas as they watched their daughter in the parish hall. And I remember the sense of teenage bitterness I felt that night when we sang, ''Twas the curse of emigration left you here my Noreen Bawn.'

The Streets of Laredo

He was like a breath of fresh air when he joined our small dance band in the early Fifties. He seemed to be the man who had everything; young, goodlooking and with a warm tenor voice. At football when he went up for a high catch, they said he came down with snow on his heels. In the mowing season when we left him home in the early hours of the morning, he would change his clothes and go straight out on the tractor to mow, as they say, 'on the country'.

In the band he would take the big double bass out to the front of the stage. He would spin it around, slap it, ride it like a horse, pretend to put it under his chin. A crowd would gather round to watch and to laugh at his antics. The song he sang best was 'The Streets of Laredo' and dancers would always stop to listen to him.

> *As I walked out in the streets of Laredo*
> *As I walked out in Laredo one day*
> *I spied a young cowboy dressed up in white linen*
> *Dressed up in white linen as cold as the clay.*

And we would come in, harmonizing the chorus. A girl said to me one night, 'Wouldn't it nearly make you cry?'

And then suddenly he left. I was told in that tactful country way that 'he wasn't well' and that 'the story was bad'. I shouldn't have gone to see him in hospital. His hair seemed too big for his grey twenty-five-year-old face, and when he shook hands with me, his arm outside the blanket was as thin as the neck of a double bass.

The old priest spoke well at his funeral. 'Death mowed him down,' he said. 'Collected him like a loose ball.'

I played the wheezy old harmonium and brought along a choir of schoolchildren to sing. Everybody said that their young voices were sweet and moving. But when they had clattered down the gallery stairs, and the chapel was empty, I saw through the edge of the stained-glass window the crowd by his grave, gathered for him again, and I started to play on the harmonium his song, the one that would nearly make you cry. But after a few bars I stopped and just sat there, thinking of the words.

So beat the drum slowly, and play the pipe lowly
Beat the dead march as you carry me along
Take me to the valley and lay the sod o'er me
For I'm a young cowboy and I know I've done
  wrong.

'Life slipped between the bars . . .'

The poet Patrick Kavanagh writes about a young country-man who doesn't notice the years passing:

> *Sitting on a wooden gate*
> *He rode in daydream cars*
> *But while he caught high ecstasies*
> *Life slipped between the bars*

It was a bit like that for me in the band. I didn't notice the changes at first, members getting married and leaving, the world of entertainment changing, a brash new generation demanding much more than we could give. The seeds for the ultimate demise of the band were sown as far back as 1955 when Bill Haley introduced Rock and

Roll for the first time with his recording of 'Rock Around the Clock'. It was very simple music, with a few basic chords and a strong back beat on the drums. The lyrics were not important, but it was fresh, wild and exciting. It was also not our style. Our forte was melody, not rhythm. We could even make a passable attempt at Glenn Miller. But we had no guitars to supply the driving beat now required.

Probably the reason that we had survived so long was that the audiences we played to came largely from similar backgrounds to our own and were not in the forefront of any move for change. We were a band of our time, and by 1962 our time was over. Life had slipped between the bars.

In the last of the diaries that John Joe kept so meticulously, he has written in green ink, on 27th May 1962, two words: 'Band ended'. The venue was Ballinamuck in the County Longford. Even after all these years, I found it poignant in its simplicity, and as I thumbed through the subsequent pages of the diary, I saw the bookings that would now never be fulfilled all ticked off as John Joe wrote, saying the band was no more.

I would love to be able to relate how the band went out in a blaze of glory with one last wonderful night's dancing. But it wasn't like that at all. We ended 'not with a bang but a whimper.' And the strange thing was, we could see it coming. It was a wet miserable night. The crowd was small and apathetic and we played badly. It was a relief to get off the stage. We didn't even wait for supper, just packed our equipment into the van and headed home over the wet and winding roads of Longford and Leitrim and Cavan.

I remember coming home on that last night. There was little drama. I was left home last of all and when the driver turned the van at our gate, he got out and so did I. We said nothing for quite a while, just stood there in our band uniform in the drizzling rain. Then he said, 'Well . . . that's the end of the Starlight.'

I said, 'It is . . . It is.'

We shook hands. He got into the van and drove away and I stood watching his tail lights disappear over Lynam's hill for the last time.

Foresight

A local man wrote an excellent history of the football club I used to play for. He went to great trouble to trace all the men who had played for it down the years and he even included their photographs with pen-pictures underneath. 'Fast nippy corner forward who gained well-deserved county honours.' 'Tall high-fielding full-back, a rock in the defensive line.'

But when it came to my picture, he wrote, 'Strong and determined. Always gave of his best.' A polite way of saying that I was utterly devoid of footballing skill of any shape, make or description. And indeed it was true. I had all the coordination and ball-control of a supermarket trolley. I spent a lot of the time on the field going around, as one spectator put it, 'Like a bull in a mist.' But the team was always short of players and I kept my place because I was physically big and sometimes managed to get in the way of opponents. On our team at that time was a character nicknamed the Clogger. He was broad, squat and fearsome. He used to make declarations of intent to the opposing forwards before the match began.

'First man that crosses the fourteen-yard line gets his leg broke. Put one foot in that square and you'll get a box on the mouth.' He was aptly named.

One day I was playing as a half-back and my immediate opponent was the type I had come to dread, small, fast and skilful. Three times in the first half he beat me to the ball, dummied inside and sent the ball over the bar leaving me floundering. Worse still, he called me 'a big awkward hallion' and defied me to get near him.

At half-time the Clogger called me over. 'This lad I'm on isn't much good,' he said. 'Me and you will swap places. I'll slow that boy down, I'll give him a good kick in the privates.' Except he didn't use the word 'privates'.

We swapped opponents. Early in the second half, the ball was kicked over the sideline and I went to fetch it from behind the whins. When I came back I could see that there was a commotion on the field. I placed the ball for the sideline kick and when I looked again, I could see my erstwhile opponent standing apparently unconcerned some distance away, and it was the Clogger who was being carried off, tenderly clutching his testicles.

Big Tom

It was said that the reason the Harps football team had won twenty-eight games in a row was because the parish priest had blessed the ball and said that they would keep on winning as long as no one told about it. When the team ran on to the field they were called the hen and the flock of chickens, because they were small and fast except for Big Tom.

When I got to know him he was middle-aged and his great strength was gone but he still possessed the massive frame and huge shoulders that had given him his nickname. In his youth he had been noted for his great feats of strength. For a bet, he had once placed his hand palm upwards on the floor of a public house, asked a man of nineteen stones to stand on it and then lifted him on to the counter with one hand. Once, like Hercules with the Nemean lion, he had choked to death a huge fox that he had caught killing the hens in the henhouse.

On the football field he was famous for the power of his shot. It was said that a man who had blocked one of his kicks had got his ribs broken. Once the goalkeeper of the opposing team had taken one look at him coming with the ball and then had run in fear sideways out of the goal to escape. Try as I might, however, I could never get him to talk about his youth, and he would never say if the story about the parish priest was true.

One day he was rucking the hay in the river meadow and I called in to give him a hand. He laughed at my unskilled efforts but as always he seemed glad of the company. When we had the meadow raked clean and the shadows of the rucks were lengthening, we sat down with our backs against one of them and he put his jacket loosely around his shoulders as countrymen do, and got out his pipe and plug tobacco. In answer to yet another question, Tom started talking, almost to himself.

'The furthest we ever got was to the county final,' he said. 'We drew with Enniskillen but in between that and the replay, three of the team emigrated to America.' As he cut and teased the tobacco, filled the bowl of the pipe and cleaned out the stem with a long stiff cushog of grass, he told me the story.

There was an American wake for them the night before

they left, with dancing and drinking and singing. One man who couldn't speak very well, under the influence of strong drink and stronger emotion, decided he would make a speech. He concluded by saying, 'The Harps will nuver play agether again.' Everyone smiled indulgently at his mispronunciation. But then they drank deep and were silent for they realized that what he said was the truth.

The next day, the emigrants and their families travelled by car to Enniskillen station where they would board the train to take them to Derry to join the great ocean liner that called there on its way from Liverpool to New York. Tom and some members of the team cycled in to see them off.

They gathered on the platform, shook hands with their comrades and then stood awkwardly in a bunch some distance away as the families said their goodbyes. The three young men got into the carriage and put their suitcases up on the rack. The guard closed the door, but they couldn't manage the strap to open the window and they sat awkwardly looking out, separated by a glass pane from their families, but already gone from them, wanting to get it over with, hoping the train would start.

Two of the mothers were weeping in great heaving sobs, the third stood perfectly still with her chalk-white face expressionless, the men standing awkward in their good suits. The guard's whistle blew an echoing warbling blast ('like the referee blowing full time,' Tom said). A huge cough of steam escaped from the engine and the whole train shuddered. Then with long, slow puffs it started moving. The younger brothers and sisters ran along the platform waving but then they too stopped and the little crowd on the platform stared silently after the train as it picked up speed and disappeared around the long curve in the cutting outside Enniskillen station. All this Tom told me, the puffs of his tobacco smoke unconsciously mimicking those of the engine, his eyes fixed on the blue of the distant Cuilcagh mountains, but what he was seeing was a cold railway station forty years ago. The team members went for a drink afterwards but Tom cycled home alone.

'It was the longest twelve miles I ever travelled,' he said: 'When I got home I went down by that river there. It was a lovely sunny day and the birds were singing – and I thought the whole world was dead.'

'What about the replay?' I asked.

'We were bet by four points.'

'Someone must have told about the parish priest,' I said.

'Maybe, but what does it matter now? Come on, we'll gather up these tools.'

And I walked out of the field beside the big man carrying the pitchforks and the rakes effortlessly on his wide shoulders.

Sheep Can't Swim

You know that old song, 'Messing About on the River'.
Well last summer four of us were doing exactly that,
messing about on the river in my small boat, when the
diesel engine stuck in reverse gear so that it would only
go backwards. And that was how we had to get home,
going backwards. On the way, we passed a large hotel
whose grounds run down to the river bank. There was
a wedding in progress and the guests were seated in the
grounds, sipping drinks in the sunshine.

At my instigation, we decided that we would do an
impersonation of a film running backwards, so we all
sat upright, as still as statues, facing the front of the boat,
but in the opposite way to the direction in which it was
travelling. Out of the tail of my eye, I could see the guests

nudging each other, stopping with drinks halfway to their mouths and staring at the four rigid figures gliding slowly past as if they were the knights at Camelot seeing the Lady of Shalott. We felt we had done a good day's work. But it is another boating incident which stands out in my memory, and I am afraid that I didn't come out of it too well.

I was coming up the river by myself when I saw a farmer acquaintance of mine on the bank. He was waving to me and pointing. I looked and saw that there was a sheep in the river. Now sheep can swim, but after a bit, their fleece becomes waterlogged and heavy, and they drown. I turned the boat around and headed towards the animal. But when I reached out to catch it, it became frightened, and plunged away. I was still making ineffectual grabs at it when a cruiser came alongside, with a German tourist on board, sitting high up on the poop deck and drinking a glass of wine. I waved him on, but, instead, he stopped to look. He called to his wife to tell her there was a sheep in the river and the conversation went something like this.

'*Helga!*'

'*Ja!*'

'*Da ist ein Schaf im Fluss.*'

'*Ein Schaf?*'

'*Ja, Helga, ein Schaf.*'

And they both watched with great interest, carrying

on an animated conversation in German as I continued to make vain attempts to capture the animal. Another cruiser arrived, this time with an Englishman at the helm. The exact same process was repeated.

I waved him on. He stopped.

'Cynthia,' he called.

'Yes dear.'

'Chap here with a sheep in the river.'

'A sheet?'

'Not a sheet, dear, a sheep.'

'What's he doing with a sheep in the river?'

'I'm teaching it to swim,' I yelled back up, by now thoroughly infuriated.

'Says he's teaching it to swim, dear.'

'Good heavens!'

Eventually, I got hold of one of the curved horns and towed the animal behind the boat to the shore where the owner was waiting. But the humiliation was not yet over.

'Good man,' he said, 'it's not worth much, but it's worth more out here than it is in there.' He reached out to take it and with that he lost his footing and slid down the steep bank, up to his armpits in water while the sheep scrambled out and trotted away over the field, shaking the water out of its fleece. Entertainment over, the two cruisers continued on their way, carrying on an animated Anglo-German conversation, punctuated by backward looks at myself and my sodden friend – the man, not the sheep.

I have often wondered about the subsequent conversations that took place in the drawing-rooms of Germany and southern England when they were talking about their holiday experiences.

Must tell you about a wonderful experience we had on a cruising holiday in Ireland. Came across a chap who was actually teaching a sheep to swim. They're all quite mad over there you know.

Punting

The summer before I went to Queen's University Belfast, we started building a new house. Times were hard and to save money we ourselves made the concrete blocks for the house. With shovels we mixed the gravel and cement, (three times dry, twice wet), and in a contraption called a blocker pounded the wet concrete into rectangular blocks six inches thick. These had to be carried on wooden pallets and left in rows on a field to dry. You had to hold them out in front of you dead weight and the strain it put on your arm muscles was colossal.

I wasn't helped by the fact that working with me was a labouring man who knew every trick in the book. I was the one who had to do the mixing, the carrying, while he did things like fetching the water or opening the bags of cement. He called me 'College boy', told me I was a softie, and laughed at my blisters and my fatigue. And always after work he would challenge me to arm-wrestle. He could beat me easily. He would distract my attention and slam my arm down, or he would hold steady against my frantic efforts and then when I had tired myself out he would contemptuously down me. The work went on for weeks and the only break was on Sunday when a couple of other young lads and myself would take a boat out on to the lough and row for miles and swim and fish.

But as the summer wore on, my body toughened, until one evening he broke off in the middle of a bout of arm-wrestling and said, 'Ah sure, it's all a cod,' and I knew I had passed my finals. But I had no time to gloat because I was off to university.

As first-years we were invited to join various societies and I put my name down for the Rowing Club and ticked 'Yes' in the section where it said, 'Previous experience'. The next day there was a note asking me to report to the captain and I did. Two large chaps in blazers with crossed oars on the crest were seated at the table.

'Ah,' the captain said, 'previous experience I see. Where were you at school?'

'Enniskillen,' I replied.

'Ah yes,' he said, 'Portora,' mentioning the famous school where Oscar Wilde had been a pupil.

'No,' I said, 'I went to Saint Michael's.'

'Saint Michael's? I didn't know they had a rowing club there.'

'They don't,' I said.

'But where exactly did you row?' he asked.

'Oh, on Upper Lough Erne,' I said.

There was a puzzled silence and then a look of absolute horror crossed his face. 'Good Gad,' he said, turning to his companion, 'chap's talking about PUNTING!' And they both laughed loud and long at this idiocy and a couple of other big lads in blazers came in, and they were told, and they looked at me as if I were a sub-species of the human race. And then a few nods and winks passed between them and I could see that they were planning a further humiliation.

The biggest and broadest of them came over to the table and said, 'You have to pass a test of physical strength, you know, before you can be allowed to enter this club. Have you ever heard of arm-wrestling?'

'No,' I lied.

He explained the rules as if he were talking to a backward child. Then he took off his blazer. He was big, all right, but when I looked at his forearms I thought that they would never be able to carry a six-inch block of wet concrete over a soggy field in Fermanagh. He tried catching me unawares but my labourer friend had taught me well. I held my ground and when I felt him weaken,

223

I slammed him to the table with a lot more force than was necessary.

'Good heavens,' said the captain. 'How did you get arms as strong as that?'

'Punting,' I said. 'Punting on Upper Lough Erne.'

The Poetry Lover

The routine was always the same. His wife would open the door to my knock.

'Can I have a lift with John on the lorry to Belfast on Monday please?'

'The college boy wants a lift,' she would shout in sideways. 'Six o'clock sharp,' she would say to me, and close the door briskly in my face.

The neighbours said she was a sharp woman. They also said that *he* wouldn't wait for the pope, and more than once I watched in impotent frustration as his taillights disappeared in the direction of Belfast, while the rooks, woken by the sound of the engine, cawed in the trees overhead. But usually I made it on time.

The lorry had a maximum speed of twenty-eight miles

per hour and so it took us three and a half weary hours to get to Belfast. But what used really to infuriate me was his unvarying predictability. My eighteen-year-old mind could forecast everything he would do. When I got in, he always said, 'Is that door closed?' and that was all. At Fivemiletown chapel he blessed himself and for the next mile said his morning prayers, moving his lips silently. At the same crossroads every morning, he blessed himself again and then, with great care and deliberation he brought out a plug of tobacco and a knife, cut and teased the tobacco, filled his pipe and lit it, all the while steering with his elbows as we trundled along the twisting roads of South Tyrone.

And always, always, when we came to the town of Augher, he would look over at me and say, 'Augher, Clogher, Fivemiletown, eh?' clearly expecting an answer, and I would mutter, 'That's a good one,' or, 'Oh indeed,' but he always seemed dissatisfied.

And then one morning I said, *'Sixmilecross and seven mile round.'*

'What?' he said angrily.

'That's the rest of it,' I said, *'Augher, Clogher, Fivemiletown, Sixmilecross and seven mile round.'*

He glared at me balefully, but for the next few miles I could see that he was trying it over in his mind.

A few weeks later we gave a lift to a local woman and

when we got to Augher, *he* said, '*Augher, Clogher, Five-miletown, Sixmilecross and seven mile round.*'

And the next week I said, '*Cookstown straight and long, The drink is right but the price is wrong.*'

'What was that?' he said sharply, and I repeated it.

A couple of weeks later as we drove out of the yard, out of the blue, he said, looking straight in front of him, '*From Carrickmacross to Crossmaglen You'll get more rogues than honest men.*' And then he looked over at me to see how I would take it

I replied, '*It wasn't the men from Shercock Or the men from Ballybay, But the dealin' men from Crossmaglen Put whiskey in me tay.*' And he said, 'I never heard that bit, that's a good one.'

And then I taught him: '*Thomasina from Ballymena Could dance on her toes like a ballerina, But she married a man from Cushendall And now she cannot dance at all.*'

And he said, 'That's a great one,' and laughed chokingly through the tobacco smoke.

And one April morning as dawn whitened the drumlins of the Clogher valley, we said all the rhymes one after another, and we ended with the one about Fermanagh. '*Lisnaskea for drinkin' tea, Maguiresbridge for brandy, Lisbellaw for woppin' straw, And Derrylin's the dandy.*'

And we sat in companionable silence for the rest of the way, winding through Tyrone and Armagh to the city.

'You'll be up next week,' he said, as I got out.

'I will,' I replied.

I never spoke a word to him again. That week, he slumped over the steering wheel in the yard, dead of a massive heart attack. I was amazed at how devastated I felt when I heard it.

In the graveyard, his wife said as I shook hands with her, 'He said you were the best of crack, that you had great rhymes.' But she spoke in a puzzled, almost resentful way, and I knew she would never understand.

The new driver was just a few years older than myself, and we talked young men's talk of football and dances and girls.

But it was never the same again.

Talking to a Ghost

My uncle was fifty-three when he and his young family emigrated to New York from a hungry mountainside in North Leitrim. He had left it too late. They said that at the foot of the aeroplane steps he stopped and made an attempt to go back. Along with the good navy-blue suit, the shirt with detachable collars, the box of collar studs and the pair of light boots, he had packed his fiddle and his bow, lovingly wrapped in sheets of newspaper. But he never played it in America and it stayed in a bottom drawer in yellowing sheets of the *Leitrim Observer*. His letters were all about home with never a mention of his new life, and always, always he wanted to know what was the price of black cattle in Collooney Fair.

On the one occasion he came back, he made his way

to the house where he and my father were reared and with a pair of pliers he pulled from the kitchen wall the nail on which he used to hang his fiddle. He took it back to his New York home, hammered it into the wall there and that night, he played his favourite reel, 'The Boys of Ballisodare', and hung his fiddle on it again.

I went back to North Leitrim some years ago to visit the old house. I had been there once before as a child with my father. Now I carried my own son on my shoulders. Round a bend up a steep lane, I suddenly came face to face with an old man coming down. He stopped and looked at me and said, 'Eddie.'

'That was my father's name,' I said.

'Well if your father was made young again, that's him walking up the lane.' He spoke in that courtly way you only find in country places, and he turned round to walk back a bit with me and show me the way. He kept looking at me as if he couldn't believe his eyes.

'Would there be any chance that you would come back and do up the house?' he said. 'I would love to see someone above me on the mountain. There was smoke from all those chimneys,' he said, pointing out the ruined houses on the mountain face. 'I rambled in every one of those houses but they're all gone now.'

'Did you never think of going away yourself?' I asked.

'I never was further than Collooney Fair,' he said. 'Never further than the Fair of Collooney.'

'What about your family?' I said.

'I have a son in Philadelphia. I was out to see him last year. I have another son in Los Angeles. I went out to him the year before. It's on the far side of America. The lane's bad but it's dry underfoot. Mind the little fellow.'

Gentle regular undulations of the grass were all that marked where my uncle's garden of brown sharp-edged ridges had been. Nettles and brambles were growing up to the open doorway. The boy wrinkled his nose at the smell of the calves in the kitchen, and through the open window I could still see the nail hole in the wall and the tracks of his pliers in the flaking pink distemper. When I had seen enough I turned to go.

The old man was waiting for me at a gap in the hedge. He had a paper bag in his hands. 'There's some apples for the boy,' he said. 'My two lads always liked them. You were always a fine big man, Eddie.' And he was gone through the gap in the hedge.

I didn't know if he was sane or mad. It was a strange and unsettling conversation. In the car when I opened the bag, the apples had hard cracked skin and black spots from years of neglect, but the flesh inside was sweet and wholesome. And as my little son and I sat eating them, I realized that the old man had not spoken to me at all. He had been talking to a ghost, the ghost of a long-dead neighbour that he had met walking up a lane in Leitrim.

ACKNOWLEDGEMENTS

One of the most pleasant tasks of writing this book is offering public thanks to the many who helped it come into being.

I am deeply indebted to my wife and family, the audience for the less-than-dressed rehearsals of my stories.

To my brother Jim, who urged me on with inspirational belief and enthusiasm.

To Michael Harding, whose literary judgement was the litmus test of much that I wrote.

To Martha McCarron, who in many ways was responsible for starting my broadcasting career.

To Jackie Smyth and to Paula McGinley, on whose intuitive expertise I frequently depended.

To Sylvie Collier, who was highly skilled in distinguishing the wheat from the chaff.

To Cat Ledger, who coaxed and cajoled me into meeting deadlines.

To Ben Dunn for his sensitive and gentle editing.